*The 500 Hidden Secrets of*

# MIAMI

# INTRODUCTION

This book invites you to discover the less-traveled causeways of Miami. The main objective is to point the reader to places that are not usually included in tourist guides, like the nut milk bar located in a Texaco gas station, or the boutique of a designer who is a stylist for hip-hop celebrities as well as a reality TV star. It also lists the most interesting galleries, museums, and other cultural institutions that Miami has to offer. It even includes some unusual experiences, such as swimming in a freshwater Venetian pool, or day trips to the Everglades and the Keys, where visitors can commune with alligators and dolphins.

The guide reflects the fascinating shift that has occurred in Miami in the last decade. South Beach and other parts of Miami Beach made their comeback starting in the early 1990s, and now also Brickell/Downtown and the MiMo District/Upper East Side thrive as neighborhoods in which to live and work. In between, Wynwood, Midtown and Miami Design District have become known as arts, dining and shopping regions. The addresses chosen echo this change, but other parts of sprawling Miami-Dade County have not been neglected.

Finally, this guide cannot possibly mention everything there is to see and do; indeed, there's always something new popping up, and something to mourn that's closed. While continuous reinvention is one of Miami's charms, it also means that this guide can only be a starting point for the discovery of this 'Gateway to the Caribbean'.

# HOW TO USE THIS BOOK?

This guide lists 500 things you need to know about Miami in 100 different categories. Most of these are places to visit, with practical information to help you find your way. Others are bits of information that help you get to know the city and its habitants. The aim of this guide is to inspire, not to cover the city from A to Z.

The places listed in the guide are given an address, including the neighborhood (for example Brickell or Pinecrest), and a number. The neighborhood and number allow you to find the locations on the maps at the beginning of the book: first look for the map of the corresponding neighborhood, then look for the right number. A word of caution however: these maps are not detailed enough to allow you to find specific locations in the city. You can obtain an excellent map from any tourist office or in most hotels. Or the addresses can be located on a smartphone.

Please also bear in mind that cities change all the time. The chef who hits a high note one day may be uninspiring on the day you happen to visit. The hotel ecstatically reviewed in this book might suddenly go downhill under a new manager. The bar listed as one of the 5 places where the rhythm is gonna get you might be empty on the night you visit. This is obviously a highly personal selection. You might not always agree with it. If you want to leave a comment, recommend a bar or reveal your favorite secret place, please visit the website *www.the500hiddensecrets.com* – you'll also find free tips and the latest news about the series there – or follow *@500hiddensecrets* on Instagram or Facebook and leave a comment.

# THE AUTHOR

Jen Karetnick has lived in Miami since 1992. As a lifestyle journalist for various outlets and food critic for *MIAMI Magazine,* she has prowled from canals to causeways, eating and drinking all the way. As a poet and author/editor of more than a dozen books and anthologies, she has observed the views and examined the wildlife from beaches to Everglades, and taken in the cultural highlights during Miami's sweeping Renaissance. As the caretaker of 14 mango trees, she has written the cookbook *Mango* (2014). And as the mother of two nearly grown children and a creative writing educator for grades 6 to 12, she has participated in whatever exciting opportunities have come along.

The author would like to thank her husband, Jon; their kids, Zoe and Remy; and their peers and friends. She would also like to thank her journalism students at Miami Arts Charter School, who helped provide the addresses, phone numbers and websites, and Raul Perdomo for his expertise in the local art scene. She is particularly grateful to Maria del Carmen Martinez, for her knowledge of Cuban everything and for keeping her son fed during soccer season. Soccer parents Michaela Bittner, Minoosh Farhangi, Tony Cervone and Suzanne Sponder also assisted with after-match research and companionship. Stacy Shugerman, as always, was game to go anywhere and do anything.

Enormous thanks to photographer Valerie Sands for tackling the project with her signature humor and revealing Miami in all its modes and moods. Additional gratitude goes to the public relations personnel, chefs, business owners and staffs who coordinated with her. Finally, a huge thank you to Dettie Luyten and her team at Luster for seeing the enchantment in the 'Magic City' and making the Miami book a firm reality.

# MIAMI (NORTH)

## overview

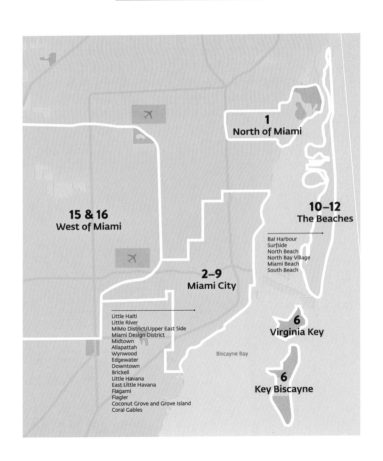

**1**
North of Miami

**15 & 16**
West of Miami

**10–12**
The Beaches

Bal Harbour
Surfside
North Beach
North Bay Village
Miami Beach
South Beach

**2–9**
Miami City

Little Haiti
Little River
MiMo District/Upper East Side
Miami Design District
Midtown
Allapattah
Wynwood
Edgewater
Downtown
Brickell
Little Havana
East Little Havana
Flagami
Flagler
Coconut Grove and Grove Island
Coral Gables

Biscayne Bay

**6**
Virginia Key

**6**
Key Biscayne

# MIAMI (SOUTH)

## *overview*

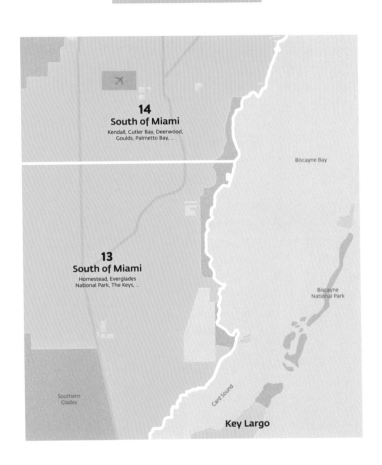

**14**
**South of Miami**
Kendall, Cutler Bay, Deerwood,
Goulds, Palmetto Bay, ...

Biscayne Bay

**13**
**South of Miami**
Homestead, Everglades
National Park, The Keys, ...

Biscayne
National Park

Southern
Glades

Card Sound

**Key Largo**

# Map 1
# NORTH OF MIAMI

EAT — **DRINK** — SHOP — BUILDINGS — DISCOVER — **CULTURE** — CHILDREN — SLEEP — WEEKEND — RANDOM

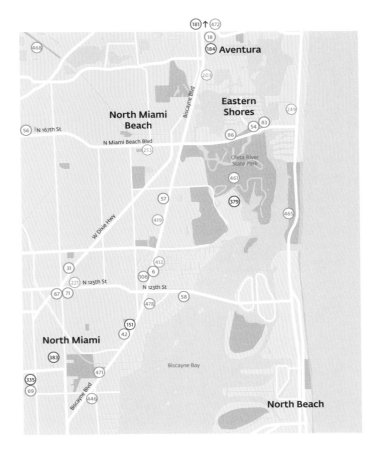

181 ↑ 472
18
184 **Aventura**

468

203

**North Miami Beach**

Biscayne Blvd

**Eastern Shores**

249

56 N 167th St

54 83
86

N Miami Beach Blvd
253

Oleta River State Park

461

57

379

465

419

W Dixie Hwy

31
412
6
221 N 125th St
106
67 71
N 123th St
478
58
151
42

**North Miami**

383

471
335
69
Biscayne Blvd
446

Biscayne Bay

**North Beach**

# MIAMI CITY

## OVERVIEW

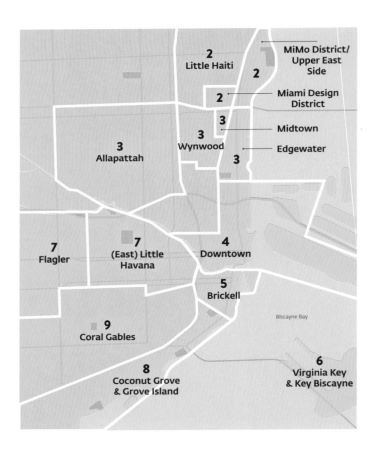

**2** Little Haiti

MiMo District/ Upper East Side

**2**

**2** Miami Design District

**3** Midtown

**3** Wynwood

**3** Edgewater

**3**

**3** Allapattah

**7** Flagler

**7** (East) Little Havana

**4** Downtown

**5** Brickell

Biscayne Bay

**9** Coral Gables

**8** Coconut Grove & Grove Island

**6** Virginia Key & Key Biscayne

# Map 2

## MIAMI CITY

### LITTLE HAITI, LITTLE RIVER, MIMO DISTRICT/UPPER EAST SIDE and MIAMI DESIGN DISTRICT

# Map 3

# MIAMI CITY

### MIDTOWN, ALLAPATTAH, WYNWOOD and EDGEWATER

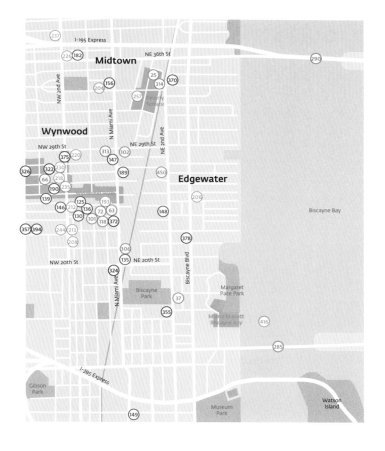

# Map 4

# MIAMI CITY

## DOWNTOWN

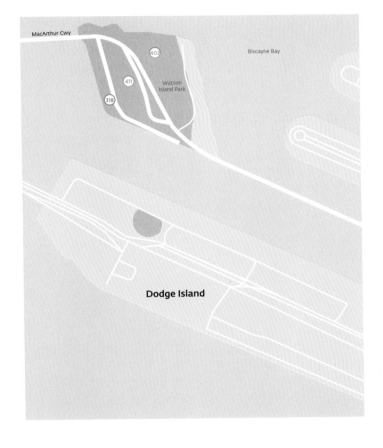

MacArthur Cwy

Biscayne Bay

402

411

318

Watson
Island Park

**Dodge Island**

# Map 5
## MIAMI CITY
### BRICKELL

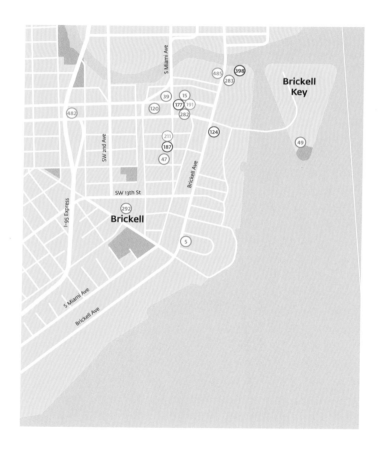

# Map 6

# MIAMI CITY

## VIRGINIA KEY *and* KEY BISCAYNE

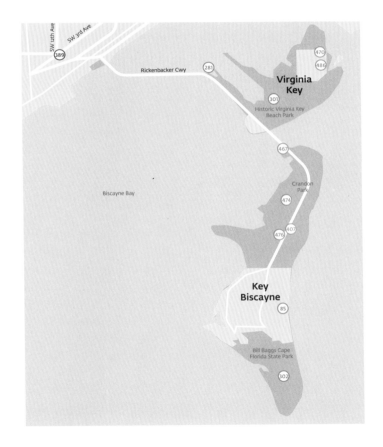

# Map 7

# MIAMI CITY

## LITTLE HAVANA, EAST LITTLE HAVANA, FLAGAMI *and* FLAGLER

# Map 8

## MIAMI CITY

### COCONUT GROVE and GROVE ISLAND

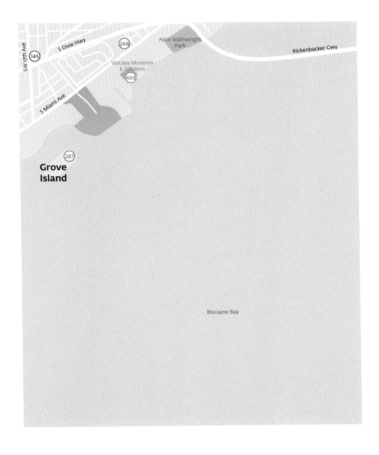

# Map 9

# MIAMI CITY

## CORAL GABLES (NORTH)

# CORAL GABLES (SOUTH)

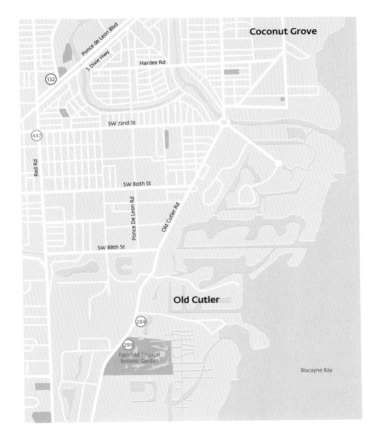

Coconut Grove

Ponce de Leon Blvd

S Dixie Hwy

Hardee Rd

132

SW 72nd St

447

Red Rd

SW 80th St

Ponce De Leon Rd

Old Cutler Rd

SW 88th St

Old Cutler

284

299
Fairchild Tropical
Botanic Garden

Biscayne Bay

# *Map 10*

# THE BEACHES

## BAL HARBOUR, SURFSIDE, NORTH BEACH *and* NORTH BAY VILLAGE

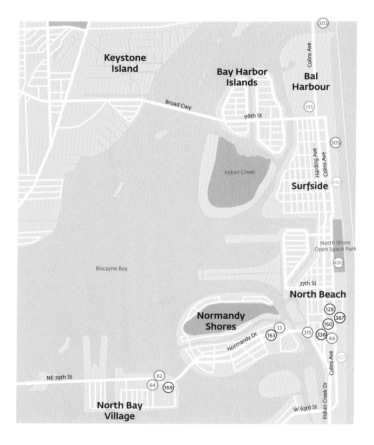

# Map 11

## THE BEACHES

### MIAMI BEACH

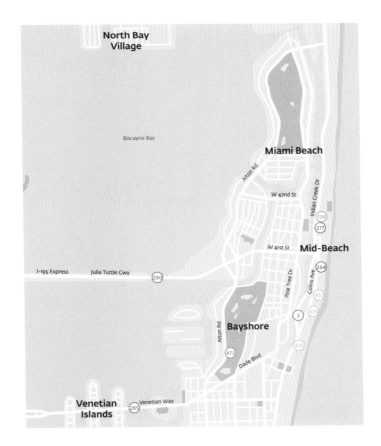

# Map 12

## THE BEACHES

### SOUTH BEACH

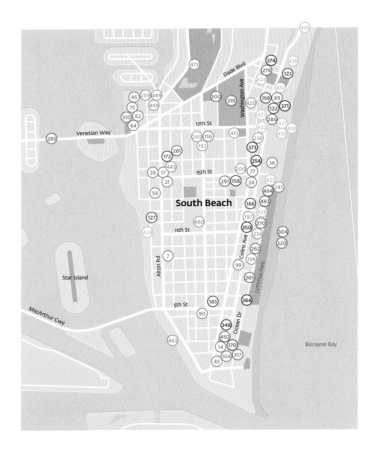

# Map 13

## SOUTH OF MIAMI

### HOMESTEAD, EVERGLADES NATIONAL PARK, THE KEYS...

# Map 14

# SOUTH OF MIAMI

## KENDALL, CUTLER BAY, DEERWOOD, GOULDS, PALMETTO BAY, ...

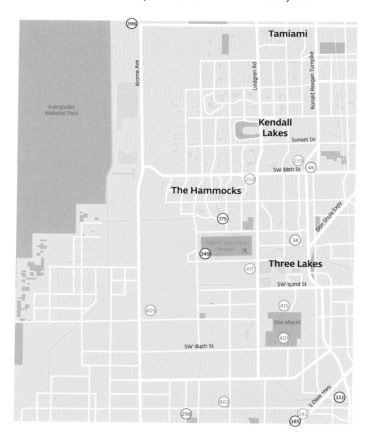

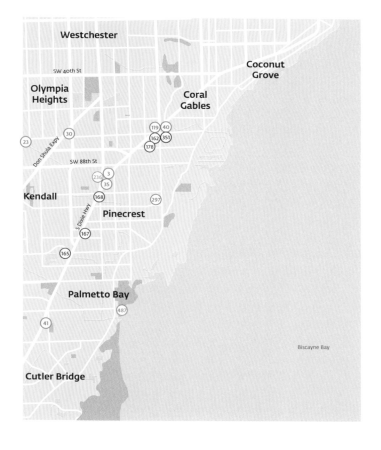

# Map 15

## WEST OF MIAMI

### MIAMI SPRINGS, WEST MIAMI, SWEETWATER, UNIVERSITY PARK, ...

Miami Springs

Doral

Miami International Airport

Westchester

Tamiami Park

University Park

# Map 16

## WEST OF MIAMI

### DORAL and HIALEAH

LIGHTKEEPERS

# 120 PLACES TO EAT OR BUY GOOD FOOD

---

# The 5 most fabulous
# FARM-TO-TABLE
## restaurants

---

1 **MICHAEL'S GENUINE FOOD & DRINK**

130 NE 40th St
Miami Design
District ②
+1 305 573 5550
*michaelsgenuine.com*

James Beard Award-winning chef-owner Michael Schwartz brings the best of the Homestead and Redland regions to this place that started it all. Fruitful pleasures for the palate include raw oysters with orange mignonette, kale pizza with goat milk ricotta, and wood oven-roasted whole snapper with lemon and roasted fennel.

2 **BOIA DE**

5205 NE 2nd Avenue
Little Haiti ②
+1 305 967 8866
*boiaderestaurant.com*

Brought to life by chef couple Luciana Giangrandi and Alex Meyer, this 24-seat spot in a strip mall is so hyper-local and seasonal that even the bread, coffee, and ice cream come from neighborhood artisans. *Boia de* means Oh My! in Italian, and that moniker is apt – every dish is worthy of an exclamation.

3 **GHEE INDIAN KITCHEN**

8965 SW 72nd Place
Kendall ⑭
+1 305 968 1850
*gheemiami.com*

Chef-owner Niven Patel's Ghee is a family-and-farm affair. His parents and wife work in this sophisticated eatery that highlights their Gujarat (western India) roots, and which utilizes the produce that's grown at their Homestead home. You can't get a more direct route to seasonal Indian cuisine.

### 4 27 RESTAURANT & BAR

AT: FREEHAND MIAMI
2727 Indian Creek Dr
Miami Beach ⑪
+1 786 476 7020
*freehandhotels.com/
miami/27-restaurant*

The focus at this foodie counterpart to the famous Broken Shaker is obvious: Local Catch Crudo. Paradise Farms Oyster Mushrooms. Florida Middleneck Clams. In fact, much of the produce is grown right outside in the gardens, then flavored with influences from owners Gabe Orta's and Elad Zvi's South American and Middle Eastern cultures.

### 5 DOCE PROVISIONS

541 SW 12th Avenue
Little Havana ⑦
+1 786 452 0161
*doceprovisions.com*

Chef-owners Justin Sherrer and Lisetty LLampalla take local sources for both raw and artisanal product, fuse them together, and serve them up. And this is how we get fried chicken on a plantain waffle with pickled peppers, Redland guava and *sriracha* honey, among other hip, Latin-influenced delicacies.

1 MICHAEL'S GENUINE FOOD & DRINK

# 5 beloved
# CUBAN
## *restaurants*

---

**6 LITTLE HAVANA RESTAURANT**

12727 Biscayne Blvd
North Miami ①
+1 305 899 9069
*littlehavana
restaurant.com*

From ham *croquetas* and *maraquitas* (plantain chips with garlicky mojo) to main courses of *lechon asado* (roasted pork) and *picadillo* (ground beef) with Creole sauce, the classics are all represented at this long-standing favorite. Formally dressed servers are quick to greet families and serve Cuban rolls.

**7 DAVID'S CAFE CAFECITO**

919 Alton Road
South Beach ⑫
+1 305 534 8736
*davidscafecafecito.com*

Originally two popular locations in South Beach, David's is now one in an entirely different spot. But it's the same great, casual diner fare. Known for fresh, hot breakfasts and *café con leches* – as well as crunchy Cuban sandwiches – this second generation-run restaurant continues to welcome the community.

**8 ISLAS CANARIAS RESTAURANT**

13695 SW 26th St
Tamiami ⑮
+1 305 559 6666
*islascanarias
restaurant.com*

Owned and run by the Garcia family since 1977, Islas Canarias is as dependable as thunderstorms in the tropics. Cuban and Spanish dishes include a homemade *tamal*, yellow rice with chicken and sweet plantains, and meatballs Catalan style, served with rice and house-cooked potato chips.

9 **LA FRAGUA RESTAURANTE**

7931 NW 2nd St
Flagami ⑦⑮
+1 305 266 3226

Much-loved Quintin and Maria Teresa Larios used to own Casa Larios, and supplied the recipes for the Estefans' Larios on the Beach (they're no longer affiliated). They returned in 2016 near the Miami International Airport, making the cream of malanga soup and *vaca frita* (fried steak) that enchanted from the beginning.

10 **ESTEFAN KITCHEN**

140 NE 39th St, #133
Miami Design
District ②
+1 786 843 3880
*estefankitchen.com*

Emilio and Gloria Estefan have been running restaurants in Miami almost as long as they've been making music in it. This one has the high-style vibe you'd expect, along with soul-stirring beats. Try the bacon-wrapped *maduros* (sweet plantain) with white cheese and guava cream for a cultural explosion on the palate.

7 DAVID'S CAFE CAFECITO

# 5 superb
# STEAK HOUSES

---

11 **EDGE STEAK & BAR**
AT: FOUR SEASONS
HOTEL MIAMI
1435 Brickell Ave
Brickell ⑤
+1 305 381 3190
*edgerestaurant
miami.com*

With its farm-to-table sourcing by chef Aaron Brooks and rooftop location – where you're warmed by fire pits when the cool winter weather sets in – the restaurant would never strike you as a corporate entity if you didn't have to go through a hotel lobby to get here. Delicacies include Wagyu beef from Australia and America.

12 **FIORITO**
5555 NE 2nd Ave
Little Haiti ②
+1 305 754 2899
*fioritomiami.com*

This charming Argentine spot, run by a trio of brothers, serves a tempting breaded steak Milanesa, topped with ham, tomato sauce and mozzarella. The Rioja-braised short ribs, which arrive with a fried egg, rival only the skirt steak with *chimichurri* for your attention.

13 **LAS VACAS GORDAS ARGENTINE STEAK HOUSE**
933 Normandy Drive
Normandy Isle ⑩
+1 305 867 1717
*lasvacasgordas.com*

Since 1996, this Argentine steak house has been serving steaks, short ribs and sausages grilled to perfection. Ask for the ever-popular *enrollada* (the rolled over), a steak weighing 0,68 kilograms that is also available as veal or as Kobe beef. Or sample a platter of mixed sausages for two. It's all *espectacular*!

## 14 RED, THE STEAKHOUSE – MIAMI BEACH

119 Washington Ave
South Beach ⑫
+1 305 534 3688
redthesteakhouse.com

Chef-partner Peter Vauthy is known for pushing the luxe limits at this South Beach steakhouse. The prime beef cuts are enormous and the free-range veal chops can be ordered as Marsala, Milanesa, Parmigiana or stuffed with foie gras, mushrooms, fontina and truffled Diane. There's even a 4,5-kilogram whole Alaskan king crab available.

## 15 QUINTO LA HUELLA

AT: EAST, MIAMI, 5TH FLOOR
788 Brickell Plaza
Brickell ⑤
+1 786 805 4646
quintolahuella.com

This sibling to Uruguay's famous beach restaurant features a parrilla as center-piece in the open kitchen. From this, all the Uruguayan grass-fed beef (and other good things) emanate, including the Bife Angosto, a 0,4-kilogram New York strip, and the Entrecôte, a 0,4-kilogram rib eye.

11 EDGE STEAK & BAR

# 5

# LATE-NIGHT/EARLY-MORNING SPOTS

---

16 **YAMBO RESTAURANT**
1643 SW 1st St
East Little Havana ⑦
+1 305 649 0203

Hearty and filling Nicaraguan food is welcome at any time of the day or night, and so are you at this cheerful place. Large portions of classic dishes like grilled steak, pork with *yuca* and *gallo pinto* (red beans and rice) for almost ridiculously low prices. Pick up after clubbing in Little Havana. Open 24/7.

17 **PINECREST BAKERY**
1511 Alton Road
South Beach ⑫
+1 786 717 5958
*pinecrestbakery.com*

A Cuban bakery open 24/7? It doesn't get better than that. Pinecrest has multiple locations, but many also have restaurants and bars, and feature eats like burgers and pizza. For that reason, we prefer the Bakery & PB Burger Joint on South Beach, given that's where the all-night party's happening anyway.

18 **BAGEL COVE RESTAURANT & DELI**
19003 Biscayne Blvd
Aventura ①
+1 305 935 4029
*bagelcove.com*

When you just gotta have an everything bagel with whitefish salad, a chili-cheese hot dog, or a pastrami sandwich at 3 am, well, now you can. An extensive menu is available for ordering for pick up through the take-out, delivery or dining in the restaurant or on the patio 24/7.

## 19 CHICO'S RESTAURANT

4070 W 12th Avenue
Hialeah ⑯
+1 305 556 8907

A Miami classic for juices, *batidos* (fruit milkshakes), *café Cubano*, and every conceivable Cuban dish. Specialties include a hefty combo plate – the Potpurri Criollo, which provides pork, white rice and black beans, a *tamal, yuca* and *croquetas*. Note: It's easy to get lost here at night if you're unfamiliar with the region.

## 20 MOSHI MOSHI

7232 Biscayne Blvd
MiMo District/
Upper East Side ②
+1 305 751 2114
*moshimoshi.us*

Congenial, cozy and open until 5 am daily, this Japanese restaurant offers a range of good eats, from perfectly prepared sushi to noodle soup bowls as big as your head. Try some rarely seen dishes, such as Tako Yaki, octopus 'pancakes' with bonito flakes, and Kimchee Buta, pork sauteed with kimchee.

# 5

# ITALIAN

*restaurants that make fresh pasta*

---

21 **VIA EMILIA 9**
1120 15th St
South Beach ⑫
+1 786 216 7150
*viaemilia9.com*

A woman sits at the window of this market-restaurant dedicated to Emilia-Romagna, but not for the view. The light helps her to see as she hand-rolls, stuffs and molds tortellini, ravioli, cappellacci and fazzoletti for Chef Wendy Cacciatori to cook, sauce and serve.

22 **RISTORANTE FRATELLI MILANO**
213 SE 1st St
Downtown ④
+1 305 373 2300
*ristorantefratelli
milano.com*

Twin brothers and chefs Roberto and Emanuele Bearzi made this eatery a destination long before downtown was revived. Their success is due, in part, to Emanuele's facility with dough, resulting in dishes as dainty as Fettuccine allo Scoglio (with seafood) and as filling as Bucatini San Babila (with Italian sausage and broccoli).

23 **OSTERIA VECCHIO PIEMONTE**
10480 SW 72nd St
Kendall ⑭
+1 786 542 5178
*osteriavpsunset.com*

This white table-cloth restaurant offers sophisticated, housemade stuffed pastas such as *agnolotti* in braised beef sauce as well as ravioli with ricotta, pumpkin and amaretti cookies in butter-sage sauce. Given the skill level, polite service and plate arrangements, prices are surprisingly reasonable.

### 24 PANE & VINO LA TRATTORIA

1450 Washington Ave
South Beach ⑫
+1 305 535 9027
*paneevinomia.com*

Charming and pastoral in décor and intention, this authentic Italian eatery nevertheless buzzes with a nightlife vibe thanks to its wine bar. Pair the select Italian bottlings with any of the inventive handmade pasta dishes, including ravioli stuffed with mushroom and shrimp, or *cavatelli* topped with fried eggplant and dry ricotta.

### 25 SALUMERIA 104

3451 NE 1st Ave, #104
Midtown ③
+1 305 424 9588
*salumeria104.com*

Technically a shop and trattoria for cured meats and cheeses, this Midtown eatery also serves terrific pastas – especially if you factor in those meats and cheeses. Housemade gnocchi with Parmigiano-Reggiano and prosciutto, for example, or Ravioli San Daniele with prosciutto, peas and cream sauce are ideal follow-ups to a selection of salumi.

21 VIA EMILIA 9

# The 5 hottest
# CARIBBEAN
## *restaurants*

---

### 26 JIMMY'Z KITCHEN

1542 Alton Road
South Beach ⑫
+1 305 534 8216
*jimmyzkitchen.com*

Chef-owner Jimmy Carey inserts Puerto Rican specialties such as *mofongo* in Miami's Cuba-heavy map. Try this plantain-based dish with a choice of proteins: chicken, *churrasco* (steak), shrimp or *mojo* (garlic sauce) pork. The Creole sauce that tops it makes it irresistible.

### 27 CHEF CRÉOLE SEAFOOD & CATERING

200 NW 54th St
Little Haiti ②
+1 305 754 2223
*chefcreole.com*

Chef-owner Wilkinson (Ken) Sejour has been called the 'Emeril of Haitian food'. He's especially proficient with zesty fish and seafood; you can tell by both the dishes and his restaurants' oceanic décor themes. Like the marinade, tartar sauce and *pikliz* (spicy vegetable relish). Buy them to take home or at the online store.

## 28 B & M MARKET & ROTI SHOP

219 NE 79th St
Little River ②
+1 305 757 2889

Curry goat never tasted as good as it does from this nondescript market, whose door is (literally) almost always open. Not a fan of goat? Not a problem. Guyanese owners Nafeeza and Sheir Ali, also cook up curry shrimp, jerk chicken, stew beef, oxtail and *dhal phourie* (split pea) roti.

## 29 ORTANIQUE ON THE MILE

278 Miracle Mile
Coral Gables ⑨
+1 305 446 7710
*ortanique
restaurants.com*

Award-winning, self-taught chef Cindy Hutson calls her food 'Cuisine of the Sun'. Along with her life partner, Delius Shirley (son of the late, great Jamaican chef Norma Shirley), she brings the flavors of so many islands to the fashionable plates of Miamians. Outstanding fare, with an extensive wine and cocktail list to match.

## 30 JAMAICA KITCHEN

8736 SW 72nd St
Kendall ⑭
+1 305 596 2585
*jamaicakitchen.com*

Locals rave about the enormous, price-friendly servings of jerk and curry chicken or pork at this shopping center joint, as well as the Jamaican patties. But don't let that dissuade you from trying the Jamaican-Chinese dishes such as the pork and ham *choy*, a mustard green that lends zingy flavor.

# 5

# FRESH FISH

## *market-restaurants*

---

### 31 CAPTAIN JIM'S SEAFOOD MARKET RESTAURANT

12950 West Dixie Highway
North Miami ①
+1 305 892 2812
*captainjimsmiami.com*

Although Captain Jim's seems to have gotten a bit pricier since being screened on Anthony Bourdain's Parts Unknown, you can usually be assured of a table here. This seafood market and restaurant stocks most of its inventory from its own fleet of boats. No frills, lots of visible chills laid out for viewing on ice.

### 32 GARCIA'S SEAFOOD GRILLE & FISH MARKET

398 NW North River Drive
Downtown ④
+1 305 375 0765
*garciasmiami.com*

As Cuban exilios, the Garcia family, all fishermen, started their seafood market business in 1966. In the early 1990s, they added this riverside restaurant with outdoor seating and an emphasis on island-style preparations such as conch fritters, ceviche, fish dip, fried, blackened or grilled grouper or *mahi-mahi* fillets.

### 33 LA CAMARONERA SEAFOOD JOINT & FISH MARKET

1952 W Flagler St
Little Havana ⑦
+1 305 642 3322
*lacamaronera.com*

This joint, stemming from Garcia Brothers Seafood, debuted in 1976 as a Cuban fish fry with stand-up counters. Today the place is still known for its quick service of *pan con minuta*, a fried snapper sandwich. Take-out from the market includes breaded lobster tail and fried grouper cheeks.

## 34 FRESHCO FISH MARKET & GRILL

12700 SW 122nd
Avenue, #113
West Kendall (14)
+1 305 278 3479
*freshcofish.com*

This no-frills, family-owned restaurant opened its Cortland Plaza restaurant in 2018, but they've actually been in the fish biz for more than two decades. That's why the Key West-style menu is so authentic, albeit with a little innovation on the side: You'll find everything from classic conch fritters to ceviche to a Philly shrimp cheese sandwich.

## 35 CAPTAIN'S TAVERN RESTAURANT

9625 S Dixie Hwy
Pinecrest (14)
+1 305 666 5979
*captainstavern
miami.com*

Transformed from a post office, this popular restaurant and market has been chugging along since 1971. Important items of note: Along with the fish and seafood selection, some of which come from local indie fishermen, the wine list is stellar. Tuesday is always 2-4-1 Maine lobster night.

35 CAPTAIN'S TAVERN RESTAURANT

# 5 excellent
# O Y S T E R
## bars

---

**36  LURE FISHBAR**
AT: LOEWS MIAMI
BEACH HOTEL
1601 Collins Avenue
South Beach ⑫
+1 305 695 4550
lurefishbar.com

Don't go through the main hotel lobby to get to this chic offshoot of a New York City brand. This restaurant, where the raw bar features six kinds of oysters (3 each from the East and West coast), has its own entrance. Try the oysters with pineapple relish, wasabi leaf or *jalapeño ponzu*.

**37  MIGNONETTE DOWNTOWN**
210 NE 18th St
Edgewater ③
+1 305 374 4635
mignonettemiami.com

Chef-owner Danny Serfer struck gold when he started shucking oysters in this Edgewater spot. The servers know the minute difference between each mollusk. Also available fried or Rockefeller. Lots of daily specials round out the offerings.

**38  ELLA'S OYSTER BAR**
1615 SW 8th St
Little Havana ⑦
+1 786 332 4436
ellasoysterbar.com

Much of the fare is infused with Florida influences, so even the oysters reflect it, designated as East Coast, West Coast and Gulf Coast. Beyond the raw, oysters Rockefeller incorporate uni butter and lime, and a lobster roll is served on a *medianoche* (sweet) bun with *Tajín* (chili peppers, salt and lime) mayo.

### 39 THE RIVER OYSTER BAR MIAMI

650 S Miami Ave
Brickell ⑤
+1 305 530 1915
*therivermiami.com*

The first oyster bar to take root in 2003, courtesy of chef-owner David Bracha, who has had several trend-setting restaurants since the early 1990s. Choose from a half-dozen varieties daily, from Hama Hama to Tatamagouche. Then move on to crudos, ceviches and more fresh fish and seafood, paired with moderately priced wines.

### 40 GRINGO'S OYSTER BAR

1549 Sunset Drive
South Miami ⑭
+1 305 284 9989
*gringosoysterbar.com*

Raw. Fried. Grilled. With chili butter. Topped with *andouille* sausage. Casino-style. New Orleans-style. In a po'boy. Yup, there are as many ways to eat the oysters here as there are varieties. And the staffers know every detail, from which method is preferable to the pedigrees of each variety.

37 MIGNONETTE DOWNTOWN

DAILY : CBGB / CRUDO / WHOLE FISH
WEST              EAST
FANNY BAY       BEAUSOLEIL
ROYAL MIYA     MALPEQUE
SUN HOLLOW   PINK MOON

# *The 5 best places to find*
# STONE CRABS
## *without the wait*

---

**41 GOLDEN RULE SEAFOOD MARKET AND RESTAURANT**

17505 S Dixie Hwy
Palmetto Bay ⑭
+1 305 235 0661
*goldenruleseafood.com*

Opened since 1943 and always in the same location, this intensely local spot has been serving Miami families for generations. Those families know that husband-and-wife team Pam Mullins and Walter Flores will have a trustworthy supply of stone crabs the moment that the season opens until the second it closes.

**42 BLUE RUNNER SEAFOOD**

11338 Biscayne Blvd
North Miami ①
+1 786 499 9334

Locals know this paneled truck, a family-run business, as the supplier of the freshest fish and seafood, including succulent stone crabs, in the Miami-Dade region. Patriarch Paco Fernando and his team sell them for a lot less than the restaurants do. Caveat: Cracking is do-it-yourself.

**43 MONTY'S RAW BAR**

2550 S Bayshore Dr
Coconut Grove ⑧
+1 305 856 3992
*montysrawbar.com*

A happy hour legend, this spot on the bay is best for the views, the live music and stone crabs in season. Modus operandi: Snack on a couple of claws and a few shrimp while watching the sunset and downing a beer after a hot day rather than investing in a full dinner.

## 44 FIFI'S SEAFOOD RESTAURANT

**6934 Collins Ave**
**North Beach** ⑩
**+1 305 865 5665**
*fifisseafood.com*

White table-cloths, Asian and Latin influences and artsy plating raises the bar a bit higher, but the métier is what stone crab aficionados look for: local, fresh, sustainable. Fifi's sources from Port Royal Trading Co., specializing in stone crabs from the Florida Keys.

## 45 JOE'S TAKE AWAY

**11 Washington Ave**
**South Beach** ⑫
**+1 305 673 4611**
*joesstonecrab.com*

Joe's Stone Crab is the restaurant that discovered the edible nature of these sustainable crustaceans, where diners wait hours in line for a table. But at the adjacent Take Away, claws can be packaged to go or consumed in serviceable surroundings, along with the signature accompaniments of hash browns, creamed spinach and key lime pie.

**42 BLUE RUNNER SEAFOOD**

# 5 scintillating
# CEVICHE
## sites

### 46 PISCO Y NAZCA CEVICHE GASTROBAR

8405 Mills Dr, #260
Kendall ⑭
+1 305 630 3844
*piscoynazca.com*

Referencing Peru's famous grape brandy, Pisco y Nazca produces excellent Pisco sours. Pair one with a host of vibrantly flavored ceviches and *tiraditos*, prepared by Executive Chef and native Peruvian Miguel Antonio Gomez Fernández, who was chef de cuisine for celebrity chef Gastón Acurio. Toast such high-end skills at gastropub prices.

### 47 SUVICHE

49 SW 11th St
Brickell ⑤
+1 305 960 7097
*suviche.com*

Enjoy this Peruvian specialty reinterpreted. Choose your fresh sea proteins, then your sauce, and have it tossed on the spot. There's also sushi, tartare, tataki, salads and some hot Peruvian fare for those who dislike it raw, plus a Pisco bar at which to soothe a thirst. Additional locations.

### 48 CVI.CHE 105 DOWNTOWN

105 NE 3rd Avenue
Downtown ④
+1 305 577 3454
*ceviche105.com*

Founder and native Peruvian Juan Chipoco and partner Luis Hoyos launched this hot spot in 2008, and its ultra-fresh ceviches and *tiraditos* still wow patrons with their authenticity, zing and succulence. The partners have a second site on Lincoln Road.

### 49 LA MAR BY GASTÓN ACURIO

AT: MANDARIN ORIENTAL, MIAMI

500 Brickell Key Dr
Brickell Key ⑤
+1 305 913 8358
mandarinoriental.com/
miami

This is the first Mandarin Oriental to feature a high-end Peruvian restaurant of renown. While celebrity Peruvian chef Gastón Acurio pops in, the day-to-day is done by Diego Oka, who sculpts fish into attractive, tender cubes and shavings, flavored with South American and Asian influences. Pricey, but worth every dollar.

### 50 JAGUAR CEVICHE SPOON BAR & LATAM GRILL

3067 Grand Ave
Coconut Grove ⑧
+1 305 444 0216
jaguarspot.
jaguarhg.com

One of the first Miami restaurants to modernize the way to eat ceviche – in Chinese soup spoon-size portions – this pan-Latin restaurant is a Coconut Grove mainstay. Choose from nearly a dozen beautifully designed ceviches, in several different quantities. The cooked fare is also a gorgeous affair, with influences ranging from Mexico to Brazil.

46 PISCO Y NAZCA CEVICHE GASTROBAR

# The 5 most fantastic
# **FUSION**
## *restaurants*

---

### 51 **FINKA TABLE & TAP**
AT: PLAZA ALEGRE
14690 SW 26th St
Tamiami ⑮
+1 305 227 8818
*finkarestaurant.com*

Brisket wonton ravioli with cheese sauce. Cuban fried rice, which is a mixture of shrimp, sweet plantains, pineapple, egg, onion and scallion. Owner Eileen Andrade combines Latin and Asian flavors to advantage. As for the tap, try a draft Peruvian or Korean beer, or a craft cocktail garnished with herbs from the restaurant's vertical garden.

### 52 **FOOQ'S**
1035 N Miami Ave
Downtown ④
+1 786 536 2749
*fooqsmiami.com*

Owner David Foulquier brings his Persian-French heritage to the menu, and Executive Chef Saul Ramos lends his Mexican culture and allover expertise. The result is seasonal dishes including local burrata with tomato jam and watercress, and Duck Leg Bastilla with spinach, cherries, cocoa and chili morita.

### 53 **TASCA DE ESPAÑA**
8770 SW 24th St
Westchester ⑮
+1 305 552 0082
*tascadeespana.us/home*

A fascinating duet of Spanish and Indian cuisines. Craving pulpo a la gallega (octopus) or chicken tikka masala with garlic naan? Get both! It's also surprising to see a Spanish bakery and a bazaar of Indian accessories, but it works.

## 54 FUEGO BY MANA

3861 NE 163 St
Aventura ①
+1 786 520 4082
*fuegobymana.com*

If pickled tongue *barbacoa* wrapped in soft corn tortillas, egg rolls stuffed with pastrami, or *empanadas* that spill pulled brisket tickle your palate, then Fuego has got you covered. This Latin American smokehouse and grill also offers an additional fusion feature that you might find surprising: It's 100 percent kosher.

## 55 PHUC YEA

7100 Biscayne Blvd
MiMo District/
Upper East Side ②
+1 305 602 3710
*phucyea.com*

Fo-get *pho* – although you will find an excellent one here, where Cajun influences blend into Vietnamese dishes. This indoor-outdoor spot (sit in the Lantern Garden or one of the interior rooms) succeeds with chef-owner Cesar Zapata's take on summer rolls, *baos*, and a signature noodle dish topped with a soft-boiled egg.

55 PHUC YEA

# 5 awesome
# ASIAN
## restaurants

---

56 **DUMPLING KING**

*237 NE 167th St*
*North Miami Beach* ⓘ
*+1 305 654 4008*
*dumplingking*
*miami.com*

Absolutely zero ambiance means you can concentrate on what you came for – Shanghai-style steamed soup dumplings, along with a host of other pan-fried and boiled combinations (string bean and pork; chives, pork and shrimp). Other dishes are all equally tasty and speedily served, which is helpful when there's a wait for a table.

57 **BASILIC VIETNAMESE GRILL**

AT: ARENA SHOPS
*14734 Biscayne Blvd*
*North Miami Beach* ⓘ
*+1 305 944 0577*
*basilicvietnamese*
*grill.com*

Wonderfully fresh Vietnamese fare, run by a trio of brothers, in a strip mall location. The pho and noodle dishes are always excellent, with huge handfuls of bean sprouts and basil to add in. But don't overlook other dishes from the extensive menu, like the ethereal, pan-fried crepe, and the spicy lemongrass duck.

## 58 ZAIKA INDIAN CUISINE

2176 NE 123rd St
North Miami ①
+1 786 409 5187
zaikamiami.com

Such consistently and beautifully balanced Indian cuisine from former Taj Mahal Hotel chefs that the owners had to expand to accommodate the demand. Traditional dishes abound, as do Zaika signatures: Malabari Chicken (with coconut curry), Kadale Lamb (with chick peas and roasted spices) and Balchao Shrimp (with vinegar and chilies). Will accommodate special diet requests.

## 59 DRUNKEN DRAGON

1424 Alton Road
South Beach ⑬
+1 305 397 8556
drunkendragon.com

This sexy hidden lounge, formerly a Latin market, is the only place in the city to cook Korean barbecue over tableside grills, and share Scorpion bowls while doing so (hence the name). If do-it-yourself doesn't please, look for wild and tongue-tingling pan-Asian preparations like the Banh Mi Cuban Presse, Sambal Snapper and Kimchee Carbonara.

## 60 LUNG YAI THAI TAPAS

1731 SW 8th St
Little Havana ⑦
+1 786 334 6262
lung-yai-thai-tapas.com

Go to this bona fide dive during off hours, so you can find a seat at the bar top or one of the few outside tables. Then slurp up some awesome spicy glass noodles with seafood and follow it up with a curry. Make sure to order everything from the start. Lingering is not encouraged.

# 5 necessary stops for
# SUSHI AND POKE

---

**61 DRAGONFLY IZAKAYA
& FISH MARKET**

5241 NW 87th Ave
Doral ⑯
+1 305 222 7447
*dragonflyrestaurants.
com/doral-florida*

This restaurant is full of moving parts: a market, fish counter and dining room filled with delectable options, including a passel of raw bar selections, inventive sushi, skewers from the robata grill, and a long list of cooked cuisine. Perhaps most interesting, though, is the nine-item Neck-to-Tail Tasting Menu, which changes daily.

**62 SUSHI GARAGE**

1784 West Ave
South Beach ⑫
+1 305 763 8355
*sushigarage.com*

Once an actual car body shop, Sushi Garage uses lug nuts for chopstick holders and plenty of reworked metal in its artistic koi fish design. Chef Oh also runs the more casual Sunny Poke next door. Another Sushi Garage opens winter 2019-20 in Coconut Grove.

## 63 ONO POKE SHOP

2320 N Miami Ave
Wynwood ③
+1 786 618 5366
onopokeshop.com

A cute, casual place to have a quick-service meal in between browsing trendy clothing stores and art galleries, Ono Poke is also high quality, headed up by a well-trained sushi chef. A very small menu utilizing only fresh tuna and salmon ensures reliability in your choice of bowl. Friendly counter service.

## 64 SUSHI ERIKA

1700 NE 79th St,
#100
North Bay Village ⑲
+1 786 216 7216

Sushi Erika carries on where its predecessor, Japanese Market / Sushi Deli, left off. Chef Erika, daughter of the owners of the former market that was renowned for its excellent, reasonably priced sushi, retained the clientele and adds new customers daily. Translations: Lines may be long, and the place closes at 7 pm.

## 65 POKÉBAO

153 Giralda Ave
Coral Gables ⑨
+1 786 801 1951
pokebaomiami.com

Former Makoto sous-chef Daniel Bouza assembles more than a half-dozen signature *poké* concoctions, using yellow-fin tuna, sake-cured salmon, prawn, crispy white fish and tofu. Then he takes it one step further and adds five irresistible and inexpensive *bao* buns stuffed with pork belly or chicken *vaca frita*. Impossible to walk away from here hungry.

# 5
# REGIONAL ARTISANS
## *to sample*

---

#### 66 ZAK THE BAKER
295+405 NW 26th St
Wynwood ③
+1 786 294 0876
*zakthebaker.com*

Oh, those crusty loaves of corn rye and brown bread. You can find Zak Stern's unmistakable products at local businesses, or try them out at his own Glatt kosher (no dairy) deli, which he opened right next door to his bakery. There, he house-smokes his whitefish and cures his salmon for the sandwiches.

#### 67 MIMMO'S MOZZARELLA ITALIAN MARKET, CAFÉ & CHEESE FACTORY
475 NE 123rd St
North Miami ①
+1 305 351 6826

Owner Bruno Ponce has a gold mine of mozzarella here, and it's an endless vein – you go in for one cheese and come out with five different types, including burrata, smoked, stuffed, even a Gorgonzola made from mozzarella. The cafe offers paninis and salads, too.

#### 68 AZUCAR ICE CREAM COMPANY
1503 SW 8th St
Little Havana ⑦
+1 305 381 0369
*azucaricecream.com*

The line at this Cuban creamery is always long. That's because the ice-cream flavors reflect the neighborhood's culture as well as the owner's heritage. For some, a scoop of the trademarked Abuela Maria, with jellied guava, cream cheese and Maria cookies, is frozen nostalgia. For others, it's novelty. For all, it's a treat.

## 69  PROPER SAUSAGES

9722 NE 2nd Ave
Miami Shores ①
+1 786 334 5734
propersausages.com

Proper means done right. And these sausages are exactly that, made with prime cuts and flavored with first-rate, regional ingredients. That's how you wind up with sausages such as The Wynwood Porter and The Lamb & Rosemary. Owners Danielle and Freddy Kaufmann also cook lunch to go; supply restaurants; run an online shop; and deliver.

## 70  MIAMI SMOKERS

306 NW 27th Ave
West Little Havana ⑦
+1 786 520 5420
miamismokers.com

Miami natives Andres Barrientos and James Bowers saw the lack of artisanal smoked meats in the region and set out to correct the problem. Now their charcuterie, bacon, porchetta, pulled Berkshire pork butt and more are sold wholesale to local restaurants and are also available in sandwiches and other take-out at their property.

67 MIMMO'S MOZZARELLA ITALIAN MARKET

# *The 5 best places for*
# PASTRIES

---

**71 CAFÉ CRÈME**
750 NE 125th St
North Miami ①
+1 786 409 3961
*cafecrememiami.com*

French pastries can make anyone give up on diet. Here, the luscious house-baked *éclairs* – try the coffee flavor for a little Miami influence – are rivaled by the hard-to-find Paris-Brest and a distinct strawberry Napoleon. Even if your waist can't, at only 4,95 dollars each, you can afford more than one. A second location is in Upper Buena Vista.

**72 THE SALTY DONUT**
50 NW 23rd St, #112
Wynwood ③
+1 305 925 8126
*saltydonut.com*

Unusually flavored gourmet donuts may be trendy, but they're also as necessary as self-confidence. Go on off hours to avoid the lines and try the ones that really represent Miami: the guava-cheese, the key lime pie, the *tres leches* and the Nutella. Okay, the last one doesn't rep the city, but who doesn't like Nutella? A second location is in South Miami.

### 73 KARLA BAKERY

6474 W Flagler St
West Miami ⑮
+1 305 267 9000
karlabakery.com

*Pastelitos.* Utter it and amazing, flaky puff pastries filled with sweet guava, mamey or apple will fall into your hands – all for less than one dollar each. Karla also makes *empanadas, croquetas, churros,* rice pudding or custard cups and *yemitas*, as well as Cuban breads and cakes. Multiple locations.

### 74 THE ORIGINAL DAILY BREAD MARKETPLACE

2400 SW 27 St
Coconut Grove ⑧
+1 305 856 0363
dailybreadmarket
place.com

A good *baklava* is not easy to find in Miami, let alone an entire bakery counter. But this all-in-one Middle Eastern marketplace has a plethora of pleasures, including bird's nests, *burma* pastries (pistachio or cashew), fragrant *namoura* and date- or nut-filled *mamoul* cookies. And, of course, outstanding walnut or pistachio *baklava*.

### 75 ICEBOX CAFÉ

1855 Purdy Avenue
South Beach ⑫
+1 305 538 8448
iceboxcafe.com

Icebox originally became known for its cakes that Oprah Winfrey declared some of her favorites. Two full-service restaurant locations later, owner Robert Siegmann's sweets, ranging from Almond Limoncello Cake with pistachios to Raspberry Chocolate Mousse Cake to his version of the 'Devil Dog', remain a focal point. Also available online for delivery.

# 5

# LATIN SPECIALTIES
## *to try before leaving Miami*

---

76 **FRITA**
AT: CUBAN GUYS
Villaverde Shopping
Center
3174 W 76th St
Hialeah ⑯
+1 786 507 4494
*cubanguys
restaurants.com*

The *frita* is a burger where the beef is
mixed with chorizo, then fried, topped
with skinny potato fries and onions,
and served on a Cuban roll. Sometimes
you'll see packaged potato sticks and
no onions. Which is why you want to
try it at Cuban Guys, who are specialists.
Multiple locations.

77 **TEQUEÑOS**
AT: CAFÉ CHARLOTTE
1497 Washington Ave
South Beach ⑫
+1 305 535 1522
*cafe-charlotte.com*

The cafe, which calls its fare a mix of
Argentinean and European, sprang from
a long-running bakery. So anything made
with dough here is spot on, including the
*tequeños*, which are mildly salty *queso blanco*
(white cheese) logs covered with pastry
and deep-fried. Be careful when you bite
into them – they can squirt like lemons.

## 78 PÃO DE QUEIJO
### AT: BOTECO
916 NE 79th St
MiMo District/
Upper East Side ②
+1 305 757 7735
botecomiami.com

*Pão de queijo* is a Brazilian cheese roll with an elastic quality to it. It's made with cassava, so it's gluten-free, and filled with mild white cheese similar to mozzarella. At Boteco, a spot-on Brazilian restaurant with live music, karaoke nights and futbol always on the television, it's the first item on the menu.

## 79 EMPANADAS
### AT: HALFMOON EMPANADAS
860 NE 79th St
MiMo District/
Upper East Side ②
+1 305 532 5277
halfmoon
empanadas.com

This commissary caters and supplies restaurants, but it also has a walk-up window and an exterior counter with stools. Snack on any of the savory pastries filled with ham and cheese, spinach, beef or chicken – plus signature combos like pulled pork with guava barbecue sauce – while you wait for a dozen to be packed up.

## 80 AREPAS
### AT: DOGGI'S AREPA BAR
7281 Biscayne Blvd
MiMo District/
Upper East Side ②
+1 786 558 9538
eatdoggis.com

Like pita bread made with cornmeal, these *arepas* are filled with a variety of stuffings, ranging from chicken salad to fried eggs with avocado. The restaurant is also known for its *cachapas* (corn pancakes) with cheese inside as well as *patacons*, sandwiches made with fried plantains instead of bread. Great for the gluten-intolerant. A few locations.

# The 5 most wonderful
# WATERFRONT
## restaurants

---

**81 BLACK POINT OCEAN GRILL**
AT: BLACK POINT MARINA
24775 SW 87th Ave
Homestead ⑬
+1 305 258 3918
*blackpoint
oceangrill.com*

There's nothing like snacking on smoked fish dip and peel-n-eat shrimp after a long day of boating, fishing or other water sports. This marina restaurant welcomes all come-as-you-are customers, and it'll also cook your catch as long as you've cleaned it, and give you two sides to boot for 9,95 dollars per person.

**82 SHUCKERS WATERFRONT GRILL**
AT: BEST WESTERN ON THE BAY INN & MARINA
1819 79th St
North Bay Village ⑩
+1 305 866 1570
*shuckersbarandgrill.com*

This long-running sports bar with dozens of televisions is built on an extensive dock in Biscayne Bay. Grab a platter of special grilled wings, fish tacos or a juicy burger, order some beers, and keep one eye on the game and the other on the sea. Pods of dolphins frequently play in the near distance.

**83 SEA GRILL RESTAURANT**
3913 NE 163rd St
North Miami Beach ①
+1 305 945 7555
*seagrillmiami.com*

Don your most expensive labels to dine at this lovely Greek restaurant on the Intracoastal. Then order grilled calamari stuffed with feta cheese or jumbo shrimp infused with lemon and oregano. Just be careful to not squirt it on the neighbor's 50.000-dollar Birkin.

### 84  IL GABBIANO

335 S Biscayne Blvd
Downtown ④
+1 305 373 0063
*ilgabbianomia.com*

This white-tablecloth Italian restaurant, a mainstay in Miami, has impeccable fare, with fish flown in daily and pastas cooked tableside. The view is equally as memorable, given that it's located in a high-rise overlooking Biscayne Bay. Sit on the patio and watch the boats speed toward the horizon while you dine.

### 85  LIGHTKEEPERS

AT: THE RITZ-CARLTON
KEY BISCAYNE
455 Grand Bay Drive
Key Biscayne ⑥
+1 305 365 4156
*lightkeepersmiami.com*

Overlooking the coast, this elegantly appointed restaurant offers fare that Executive Chef Raul A. Del Pozo sources from Key West to Central Florida. Try dishes that blaze through the Josper oven, such as the Caribbean spiny lobster tail with garlic confit or the Palmetto Creek pork chop with smoked chorizo and white bean ragout.

85  LIGHTKEEPERS

# The 5 best spots for
# SANDWICHES AND BURGERS

---

### 86 KABOBJI
3055 NE 163rd St
North Miami Beach ①
+1 305 354 8484
*eatkabobji.com*

If a sandwich is only as good as its bread, then Kabobji is the best around thanks to its house-made pita, which is constantly flying out of the oven. Stuffed with lamb kabob, chicken shawarma, or falafel – to name a few options – and topped with homemade tahini or garlic sauce, these wraps are wonderfully satisfying.

### 87 MS. CHEEZIOUS
7418 Biscayne Blvd
MiMo District/
Upper East Side ②
+1 305 989 4019
*mscheezious.com*

Expect oozy, cheesy goodness from any of these grilled sandwiches, which are a solid, inexpensive game plan for pre- or post-party. Some favorites: Frito Pie Melt, Croqueta Monsieur, Southern Fried Chicken and Waffle Melt. Gluten-free bread available. Counter service.

### 88 ROYAL CASTLE
2700 NW 79th St
Little River ②
+1 305 696 8241
*royal-castle.
business.site*

Once a chain with more than 175 locations, this quick-service burger joint is down to a singular unit in a neighborhood that is safer during the day but also rapidly gentrifying. It's known for small sliders, topped with grilled onions and a pickle. Inexpensive.

### 89  K RAMEN.BURGER. BEER

AT: TOWNHOUSE HOTEL
150 20th St
South Beach ⑫
+1 305 534 7895
*sbe.com/kramen*

Customers are understandably drawn to the outstanding *ramen* here. But the burger is also a signature, constructed with caramelized onion, tomato, American cheese and the kicker, the chef's piquant, creamy sauce. Come for this on Tuesday karaoke night – if you perform, your first Funky Buddha Hop Gun is on the house.

### 90  REGINA'S GROCERY

AT: URBANICA
THE MERIDIAN HOTEL
418 Meridian Avenue
South Beach ⑫
*reginasgrocery.com*

Uncle Jimmy. Cousin Vinny. Grandma Lucy. These actually were relatives of owners Roman Grandinetti and mother Regina, but now they're Italian sandwiches that you'll love like your own family members. This Miami location is the first offshoot of the famous deli in NYC, but not many know that it's here. Now you do.

87 MS. CHEEZIOUS

# 5
# RESTAURANTS THAT ARE SO MIAMI

**91  CAFÉ ROVAL**

5808 NE 4th Ct
MiMo District/
Upper East Side ②
+1 786 953 7850
*caferoval.com*

Owner Mark Soyka, who started the South Beach Renaissance with News Café, transformed this historic 1923 location into his latest indoor-outdoor success. Now this one-time pump house, made from native coral, is a design dream. Dine al fresco amidst lush landscaping on deboned yellowtail snapper with *faro tabbouleh*.

**92  SHERWOOD'S BISTRO & BAR**

8281 NE 2nd Ave
Little River ②
+1 786 359 4030

Don't be confused by the Native American references and artwork. They're meant to reference the area's connection to the Tequesta Indians (there's a burial mound close by). The reclaimed vintage floor and ceiling are oh-so-MiMo, and the fare is oh-so-modern, roaming from *ramen* to rabbit potpie.

**93  THE LOCAL CRAFT FOOD & DRINK**

150 Giralda Ave
Coral Gables ⑨
+1 305 648 5687
*thelocal150.com*

Inconspicuous from the outside, charming on the inside. This gastropub uses products that cater to the community like Zak the Baker bread and Abita root beer, plus craft beers. This place reps the Miami that residents like to keep to themselves.

## 94 MANDOLIN AEGEAN BISTRO

4312 NE 2nd Ave
Miami Design
District ②
+1 305 749 9140
*mandolinmiami.com*

In 2009, husband-and-wife team Ahmet Erkaya and Anastasia Koutsioukis reconditioned a house to fashion this mostly outdoor Greek-Turkish restaurant. You can't help but be seduced by the dips and salads, kebabs, moussaka and whole grilled fish as you dine under the large shade trees that have been there since the 1940s.

## 95 PUBBELLY SUSHI

1424 20th St
South Beach ⑫
+1 305 531 9282
*pubbellysushi.us*

Original, inventive and homegrown, this sushi gastropub launched both the Sunset Harbour neighborhood and an empire for chef-owners José Mendín, Andreas Schreiner and Sergio Navarro. Expect palate-challenging combinations like the Softshell Crab BLT or the Porkbelly & Clams rolls. Like Miami, it sounds weird but works. Several locations.

91 CAFÉ ROVAL

# The 5 best restaurants for
# SPECIAL DIETS

---

## 96 CHOICES ORGANIC CAFÉ

2895 McFarlane Rd
Coconut Grove ⑧
+1 305 414 0330
*choicescafe.com*

The percentages are in: Choices, where customers can make the right, smart ones, is 95% organic and 100% vegan. Those with dairy and wheat sensitivities can dine freely. Soy and nut allergies are also taken into account; although used in some dishes as to replace proteins and cheeses, other dishes are entirely without.

## 97 MORA PIZZA

3201 NW 7th Ave
Allapattah ③
+1 239 910 9145
*morapizzamenu.com*

We'll be honest – this isn't the most picturesque eatery. But when it comes to NYC-style vegan pizza, you won't find better. Pies like Buffalo Chicken, Barbecue Chicken, and the Bianca – topped with vegan ricotta and garlic oil – prove you don't have to dip into the dairy to eat like a real New Yorker.

## 98 ATLAS MEAT-FREE DELI

98 NE 79th St
Little River ②
+1 305 323 6661
*atlasmeatfreedeli.com*

It sounds counterintuitive, but the deli classics purveyed here – gyros, pastrami, Kansas City-style burnt tips – are all vegan. Fondly known as the 'plant butchers,' Atlas supplies those who are consuming non-meat diets with some terrific options, and adding a great deal of variety Miami's burgeoning vegan and vegetarian scene.

## 99 PLANT THEORY
### AT: THE WHITELAW HOTEL

808 Collins Ave
South Beach ⑬
+1 305 398 7000
*plant-theory.com*

This breakfast-lunch spot in the heart of South Beach is all about the healing of earth and human. The go-to items here include raw and cooked foods, which are local, non-GMO, organic and seasonal, such as dehydrated 'neatballs' with raw marinara and the 'Barbecue Guava Pulled Jackfruit' wrap. Kombucha Ice Kream Float for dessert!

## 100 VEGANAROMA ORGANIC CAFÉ

3808 SW 8th St
Coral Gables ⑨
+1 305 444 3826
*veganaromacoral gables.com/6255*

With an Italian twist, this cafe features menu items like marinated mushrooms stuffed with cashew cheese and garnished with pesto, bruschetta on toasted sprouted grain bread, pizzas served both warm and cold, and raw lasagna and zucchini pasta dishes. Mostly but not all raw.

# 5 of the best places for
# BREAKFAST
## and BRUNCH

---

## 101 LAID FRESH

250 NW 24th St
Wynwood ③
+1 305 699 0601
*laidfresh.com*

Whether you want a mug of coffee
or a mug of mimosa – and yes, that's
a thing – Laid Fresh is here for you.
Follow with an EBLT (fried egg, bacon,
lettuce and tomato), or a fried egg,
tomato and Mimmo's mozzarella
sandwich, or even just some beignets
to make your morning sweet.

## 102 MORGANS

28 NE 29th St
Midtown ③
+1 305 573 9678
*themorgans
restaurant.com*

Everybody loves this Barclay Graebner
(Sherwood's, Black Sheep) restaurant,
located in a restored house with a porch.
In a rush? Get there early to get a table.
Otherwise, since you can order the Mac
& Cheese with a sunny side egg or the
Mascarpone and Raspberry French Toast
all day, it doesn't matter about time.

## 103 NOVIKOV MIAMI

300 S Biscayne Blvd
Downtown ④
+1 305 489 1000
novikovmiami.com

Miami doesn't have nearly enough restaurants for dim sum. Fortunately, Novikov is doing its part to fix the problem by offering a three-course Sunday 'lunch' for $23. The courses include soup, dumplings and a main dish. Add dessert and a bottle of rosé; the additional stipend is well worth rounding out the experience.

## 104 PRIME FISH

100 Collins Ave
South Beach ⑫
+1 305 532 4550
mylesrestaurant
group.com

Owned by renowned restaurateur Myles Chefetz (Prime 112, Prime Italian), Prime Fish reinvents the fabulous buffet brunch from Chefetz's first South Beach eatery, Nemo. That makes sense, given that it's in the same location. Try everything from roasted beets and blue cheese salad to curried fish cakes to duck confit hash. Bottomless Bellinis, Bloody Marys and more. Saturday and Sunday.

## 105 GREENSTREET CAFÉ LOUNGE AND RESTAURANT

3468 Main Hwy
Coconut Grove ⑧
+1 305 444 0244
greenstreetcafe.net

You can get a lovely breakfast – coconut-crusted French toast, Brie omelets, eggs scrambled with asparagus or caviar – any day of the week. But weekend brunch is when you can order gluten-free pancakes, or may want to indulge in a Greenstreet Mary, made with this sidewalk cafe's own signature organic green tomato mix.

# 5 locals' favorites for
# PIZZA

---

### 106 EVIO'S PIZZA & GRILL

12600 Biscayne Blvd
North Miami ①
+1 305 899 7699
eviospizza.com

Even with a roster of specialty pizzas –
try The Gyro, with gyro meat, Roma
tomatoes, onions and tzatziki sauce – it's
the basic New York-style cheese pizza that
has folks raving about Evio's. A slice folds
just right in your hands.

### 107 'O MUNACIELLO

6425 Biscayne Blvd
MiMo District/
Upper East Side ②
+1 786 907 4000
munaciello-miami.com

Modeled after its big sibling in Florence,
this colorful establishment produces
pizzas under Pizza Master Carmine
Candito. His experience and heritage
shows in each crisp pie – including the
black pizzas that incorporate edible
charcoal – that emerges from the brick
oven, custom-made in Naples.

### 108 PROOF

AT: TAURUS BEER &
WHISK(E)Y HOUSE
3540 Main Highway
Coconut Grove ⑧
+1 305 529 6523
taurusbeerand
whiskey.com/food

Justin Flit's perfectly charred pizzas
were so beloved that when he closed his
Midtown location, fans mourned. They
then rejoiced when Taurus, the oldest
drinking establishment in Miami, invited
him to cook the pies there. Now Proof
pizzas are available Wed-Sun at Taurus, the
ideal complement to happy hour cocktails.

### 109 HARRY'S PIZZERIA

3918 N Miami Ave
Miami Design
District ②
+1 786 275 4963
*harryspizzeria.com*

Launched in 2011 by James Beard Award-winning chef Michael Schwartz and named for his son, this gourmet pizza mini-chain was the first of its kind in Miami. Varieties range from classic margherita to quirky, with toppings like slow-roasted pork, fig, fontina and arugula, or rock shrimp with roasted lemon, manchego, scallion and cilantro. Several locations.

### 110 CRUST

68 NW 5th St
Downtown ④⑦
+1 305 371 7065
*crust-usa.com*

This renovated house by the Miami River has become known for Mediterranean dishes of all kinds. But the pizza is what many diners return for, especially when craving specialties like the Grilled Octopus Pizza, layered with prosciutto, kalamata olives and roasted red peppers. Toppings abound, and gluten-free crust is available.

107 'O MUNACIELLO

# The 5 best
# TROPICAL FRUIT
## markets

### 111 EL PALACIO DE LOS JUGOS

5721 W Flagler St
Flagami ⑮
+1 305 264 8662
elpalaciodelosjugos.com

If it's in season, you'll find it at this
incredible market, which stocks every
kind of tropical fruit imaginable. Have
them juiced or blended as a smoothie.
You can also have a delicious Cuban meal.
Time in Miami is not complete without
a stop here. Nearly ten iconic locations.

### 112 ROBERT IS HERE

19200 SW 344 St
Homestead ⑬
+1 305 246 1592
robertishere.com

This fruit stand in Homestead's mango
and avocado groves has become a stop on
the tourist trail. Don't let that deter you.
On your way to Everglades National Park,
it's an ideal pit stop for a milkshake, some
ultra-fresh produce and preserves, and
an awesome Instagram image posing with
the vintage farm vehicles parked out front.

### 113 LOS PINAREÑOS FRUTERIA

1334 SW 8th St
Little Havana ⑦
+1 305 285 1135

This small, family-run, open-air market
makes fresh juices and smoothies while
you wait. Plenty of coconuts await to
be lopped off with a machete and handed
to you with a straw. There's also fresh
sugarcane, bananas, melons, mangoes,
avocados and citrus.

### 114 LA JUGUERA TROPICAL

10140 SW 56th St
Olympia Heights ⑮
+1 305 595 3488
*jugueratropical.com*

An all-in-one grocery store, *ventanita* and cafeteria allows you to shop, take out *café Cubano* and sandwiches, and even have a full meal. The produce is a lovely assortment of everything you need to eat, juice and cook with in a tropical household: citrus, bananas, sugarcane, avocado and more.

### 115 SOUTHWEST COMMUNITY FARMERS' MARKET

AT: TROPICAL PARK
7900 SW 40th St
Olympia Heights ⑮
+1 305 663 0917
*swcommunity*
*farmersmarket.org*

While much of the South Florida produce is harvested from November to May, the picking season for tropical fruits is the opposite. That's why this market is open year-round on Saturdays from 9 am to 3 pm. Stop by Farmer Fred of the Redland and Benny's Produce in particular for seasonal fruits like mangoes and avocadoes, carambola, jackfruit and bananas.

112 ROBERT IS HERE

## 5 *fantastic*
# FOOD HALLS

---

**116 THE LINCOLN EATERY**

*723 Lincoln Lane N*
*South Beach* ⑫
*thelincolneatery.com*

A couple of things make this food hall stand out from the others: 1) It's designed by Arquitectonica, who put the Miami architecture scene back on the map during the 1980s, and 2) The global vendors, which range from Thai to French to Mexican *paletas*, include three kosher concepts. The wide appeal sells.

**117 ST. ROCH MARKET MIAMI**

*140 NE 39th St*
*Miami Design*
*District* ②
*+1 786 542 8977*
*miami.strochmarket.com*

Adding tempting eats to the tug of alluring brands in the Design District, St. Roch brings its concept from New Orleans. Which means that not only is it food-centric, it's cocktail-centric as well, with the chefs and food vendors circling The Mayhaw, the craft cocktail bar. What's not to like about that?

**118 1-800-LUCKY**

*43 NW 23rd St*
*Wynwood* ③
*+1 305 768 9826*
*1800lucky.com*

The funkiest and hippest of the food halls – as befitting its artsy locale – 1-800-LUCKY was also tone of the first. It remains one of the favorites for its all-Asian concept. You can get everything here from sushi to dim sum to bubble tea, and even get in some karaoke time with friends.

## 119 YUMBRELLA

AT: THE SHOPS
AT SUNSET PLACE

5701 Sunset Drive
South Miami ⑭
+1 305 397 8499

Was Yumbrella Miami's first food hall? Back in the 1970s, yes. This revitalized version features more than a half-dozen global concepts, including Dr. Limon Express and King of Racks BBQ. The space also includes entertainment, with a stage for DJs, live bands, and karaoke opportunities.

## 120 CASA TUA CUCINA

AT: BRICKELL CITY CENTRE

70 SW 7th St
Brickell ⑤
+1 305 755 0320
brickellcitycentre.com/
whats-here/directory/
casa-tua-cucina

This high-end, attractive space includes everything you could want. Whether you're looking for fresh or imported ingredients to bring home or a meal to have on the spot, Casa Tua Cucina, designed by the same team behind the famed Casa Tua Restaurant on South Beach, has your best Italian interests at heart.

WYNWOOD BREWING COMPANY

# 70 PLACES
# FOR A DRINK

---

## 5 places where
# THE RHYTHM IS GONNA GET YOU

---

### 121 BALL & CHAIN

**1513 SW 8th St**
**Little Havana** ⑦
**+1 305 643 7820**
*ballandchain*
*miami.com*

Hugely popular on Calle Ocho, especially on weekends, this historic bar was established in 1935 as a saloon, then as a nightclub featuring live jazz. Today it's a mainstay that books acts ranging from Grammy-nominated headliners to salsa bands to DJs. Always colorful, always representative of Miami culture. No cover but often a wait; 21+.

### 122 THE CABARET SOUTH BEACH

AT: SHELBORNE
SOUTH BEACH
**1801 Collins Avenue**
**South Beach** ⑫
**+1 305 504 7500**
*thecabaret*
*southbeach.com*

Don't be surprised at this piano bar when your bartender or server takes the mic. Nearly every server here sings while delivering drinks called such whimsical names as 'The Talking Melon' and 'The Bourbon Thief'. A full dinner menu and light bites are available. Live music Friday and Saturday; no cover.

### 123 LIVING ROOM

AT: W SOUTH BEACH
HOTEL
**2201 Collins Ave
South Beach** ⑫
**+1 305 938 3000**
*marriott.com*
*wsouthbeach.com*

Grammy Award- and Latin Grammy Award-nominated musicians take the stage at this comfy, hip and colorful lobby lounge. Here you can keep a jazz, funk, pop, or country beat while you sip on creative craft cocktails and munch snacks. EDM DJs are also invited as part of the establishment's residency programs.

### 124 KOMODO LOUNGE

**801 Brickell Ave
Brickell** ⑤
**+1 305 534 2211**
*komodomiami.com*

This pan-Asian restaurant is a steady forerunner (make reservations to dine). But for music, take your Golden Geisha, Samurai Jack and Pikachu cocktails upstairs on the third floor, where owner and nightlife aficionado David Grutman books live musicians and DJs on the weekends. The names are always a surprise, but expect celebrities.

### 125 GRAMPS

**176 NW 24th St
Wynwood** ③
**gramps.com**

A favorite with the locals, Gramps features a different genre, from indie punk bands to DJs to R&B, nightly. It also features drag shows, game nights, and arts events. And to be clear, there's a warning to those who imbibe too many Gramps Old Fashioneds: Tip automatically applied to tabs left open overnight.

# 5 great
## BIERGARTENS

---

### 126 FRITZ & FRANZ BIERHAUS

**60 Merrick Way**
**Coral Gables** ⑨
**+1 305 774 1883**
*bierhaus.cc*

A mainstay, Fritz & Franz is one of the only places to celebrate Oktoberfest in Miami. Sit outside in pictographic 'City Beautiful' to enjoy your German brew and sausage platter. Or come for any soccer game, from an MLS to a Championship League match – Fritz & Franz shows them all.

### 127 BIKINI HOSTEL CAFE & BEER GARDEN

**1255 West Ave**
**South Beach** ⑫
**+1 305 253 9000**
*bikinihostel.com*

An inexpensive, international gathering place. Traveling students who stay in the hostel, and even those who don't, order buckets of beer to drink in the courtyard after a day on the beach or a night on the town. The food is also cheap and always available, from breakfast all day to late-night after-club bites.

### 128 BLUE BEER GARDEN

**7337 Harding Ave**
**Surfside** ⑩
**+1 786 830 7562**
*thenewhotelmiami.com*

This Blue Beer Garden place is actually pretty green, with organic chicken skewers, local burrata with heirloom tomatoes and veggie burgers. As for brews, there's a representative style of just about everything, from a draft blonde ale to a bottled tripel. Gluten-free? Two words: Apple cider.

### 129 BAVARIA HAUS MIAMI

AT: BAYSIDE
MARKETPLACE, N219
**401 Biscayne Blvd
Downtown** ④
**+1 786 483 8861**
*bavariahaus.us*

Whether you're into watching dolphins kick up surf or futbol players kick up turf, hang out here with a Hefe Weizen and a homemade pretzel. As a partner of Hofbräu München, the restaurant offers beer directly imported from Munich – and even puts it into the house-made gravy.

### 130 THE BUTCHER SHOP BEER GARDEN & GRILL

**165 NW 23rd St
Wynwood** ③
**+1 305 846 9120**
*butchershopmiami.com*

The beer garden, in this case, is the front courtyard, where happy hour is a densely populated Millennial ritual of craft beer consumption. Inside, a butcher shop supplies fresh-cut steaks, chops, burgers and sausages for taking home or dining there. Conceived by father-son partners Igor and Fred Niznik, the marriage charms.

# *The 5 best*

# BREWPUBS AND GASTROPUBS

---

### 131 BULLA GASTROBAR

**2500 Ponce De Leon
Boulevard
Coral Gables** ⑨
**+1 305 441 0107**
*bullagastrobar.com*

In Miami, brewpubs come in all ethnicities. Here you can get your futbol on, choose from an extensive beverage list, and nosh on both traditional and creative tapas like Iberian ham croquettes with fig jelly or the signature *huevos Bulla* (eggs, homemade chips, Serrano ham, potato foam and truffle oil). A second location in Doral.

### 132 TITANIC RESTAURANT & BREWERY

**5813 Ponce De Leon
Boulevard
Coral Gables** ⑨
**+1 305 667 2537**
*titanicbrewery.com*

The closest off-campus bar to University of Miami also happens to be the first, award-winning brewpub in Miami's history. Owner Kevin Rusk developed the concept in 1995, which was a nod to the cruise industry, not the movie. Try the local *mahi-mahi* or peel-and-eat shrimp with a Triple Screw while listening to live blues jams.

### 133 M.I.A. BRUHAUS

10400 NW 33rd St,
#150
Doral ⑯
+1 786 801 1721
*mia.beer*

Outpacing Wynwood, Doral is set to become the city's brewing center. The Bruhaus means business, too, with 54 draft lines – 12 offered year-round, the others periodically – and a wide-ranging menu. You can snack on candied bacon from Miami Smokers or get serious with *pan con bistec* or short rib mac & cheese.

### 134 THE SEVEN DIALS

2030 Douglas Road
Coral Gables ⑨
+1 786 542 1603
*sevendialsmiami.com*

Brit chef-owner Andrew Gilbert brings his gastropub know-how to the Latin, artisanal, farm-to-table scene, creating gorgeous fusion items like the 'London Particular' soup (green pea, Iberico ham broth, truffle oil) served with Zak the Baker's bread. Is it enough to say the burger is spread with marmite mayo?

### 135 KUSH

2003 N Miami Ave
Wynwood ③
+1 305 576 4500
*kushwynwood.com*

With local sourcing from just about every craft beer, farm and food artisan in the region, owner Matthew Kusher has made this tiny Wynwood storefront a hotspot. Go here for the Homestead guacamole, the Kush-branded burgers, the Proper Sausages served with fried pickles, the Gabe's Gator tacos (yep, that's alligator), and of course, the brewskis.

# 5 (mostly) beverage-only
# BREWERIES

---

### 136 J. WAKEFIELD BREWING

120 NW 24th St
Wynwood ③
+1 786 254 7779
*jwakefieldbrewing.com*

In 2005, John Wakefield started brewing as a hobby; in 2015, he made his habit his vocation. Cheers to him, and to the public who get to enjoy the fruits of his obsession: Five permanent taps including the ironically named La Nada (this one weighs in at 13%!). A host of seasonal beers means there's always something new to discover.

### 137 BISCAYNE BAY BREWING COMPANY

8000 NW 25th St,
#500
Doral ⑯
+1 305 381 5718
*biscaynebaybrewing.com*

With a theme relying on ocean voyages, the tap and barrel room, located in the production facility, is a handsome throwback to wooden sailing ships. Try a handful of core beers, including Saison, Miami Pale Ale, La Colada and Double Nine IPA, as well as seasonal offerings.

### 138 THE TANK BREWING CO.

5100 NW 72nd Ave,
Bay A1
Doral ⑯
+1 786 801 1554
*thetankbrewing.com*

Take a tour of the inner workings (book in advance online) and wind up in the tasting room. There you can imbibe the core beers on tap, including a relatively light Freedom Tower American Ale at 5,3% alcohol, along with special seasonal hop, Abbey, small batch, and limited series of brews.

### 139 CONCRETE BEACH BREWERY

325 NW 24th St
Wynwood ③
+1 305 796 2727
*concretebeach
brewery.com*

Make this a stop on your Wynwood arts-and-beer crawl, as this doubles as a gallery. It pours six rotating brews, which might include the Más Hops Double IPA or the Rosé Ale. Different events are set up in the Social Hall, which is where you can also buy more than a dozen different styles in cans, growlers, and kegs (kegs need 48 hours notice).

### 140 WYNWOOD BREWING COMPANY

565 NW 24th St
Wynwood ③
+1 305 982 8732
*wynwoodbrewing.com*

Each tap here was created by a woodturner and painted to resemble a spray paint can. Out of them pour the awardwinning Pop's Porter, named for founder Luis Brignoni Sr, and the flagship La Rubia Blonde Ale, among others, including occasional and special releases. The brewery – the first such craft establishment to open in Miami – also hosts special events.

140 WYNWOOD BREWING COMPANY

# 5

# GAS STATIONS

## *with the best eats and drinks*

---

141 **CHEVRON**
EUROPA COFFEE HOUSE
**6075 Biscayne Blvd**
**MiMo District/**
**Upper East Side** ②
**+1 305 754 2357**

An elegantly appointed convenience store, this easily accessible spot provides European-style baguette and croissant sandwiches, pastries and cakes, and coffee drinks. Relax with a tasty, no-fuss lunch or dinner while your vehicle is detailed at the car wash.

142 **WESTAR**
MIMA'S KITCHEN
**2190 SW 22nd St**
**Coral Way** ⑧
**+1 305 860 5888**
*mimaskitchen.net*

Known for the *pan con bistec* (steak sandwich) and fresh Cuban bread, Mima's is a satisfying slice of Cuba. Breakfast combos, Saturday lunch specials and live Latin music on Fridays from 4 to 7 pm make it even more tempting to stop in and fill up on classic island dishes.

143 **MOBIL**
MENDEZ FUEL
**3201 Coral Way**
**Coral Way** ⑧
**+1 305 443 2976**
*fueljuicemiami.com*

'Fuel Premium Grade Juices' are cold-pressed here and bottled. Like a road trip to the Keys, they're good for about 72 hours. You can also fill up growlers with craft beer, and the 'Good Morning Vietnam' and 'My Mother (Supa Cuban)' sandwiches are pretty awesome, too.

### 144 **EXXON**
PEPITO'S PLAZA
**10701 NW 58th St**
**Doral** ⑯
**+1 305 599 3503**

Head to the back of this unassuming gas station to find Venezuelan cuisine awaiting your palate. The Venezuelan-style burgers and hotdogs are delicious, but for something truly representative, try the *reina pepiada arepa,* which is a shredded chicken and avocado sandwich in a crispy corn-based bread. Now this is filling up.

### 145 **BP STATION**
EL CARAJO
**2465 SW 17th Ave**
**Coconut Grove** ⑧
**+1 305 856 2424**
*el-carajo.com*

On the outside, it could be any other convenience store. Inside, a whole other world exists – literally. The wine store features more than 2000 global labels. The restaurant offers everything from fried sardines to grilled skirt steak with *chimichurri.* The bakery supplies *macarons* and *cortaditos.* And it's all open 24/7.

145  EL CARAJO

# 5
# COFFEE AND
# SWEETS SHOPS

---

**146 PANTHER COFFEE**

2390 NW 2nd Avenue
Wynwood ③
+1 305 677 3952
*panthercoffee.com*

Miami's first independent coffee mini-chain has been a rousing success. It roasts its own coffee in small batches, not only supplying itself but restaurants and cafes. In its own locations, it also serves baked goods and wine, and fosters appreciation of the arts, both visual and performing. A true Miami institution.

**147 FIREMAN DEREK'S BAKE SHOP AND CAFE**

2818 N Miami Ave
Wynwood ③
+1 786 703 3623
*firemandereks.com*

Former City of Miami firefighter Derek Kaplan proves true the myth that firefighters know how to cook. He started his bakery with his perfected key lime pie, then quickly mastered others, including s'mores, chocolate pecan and multiple types of fruit pies. Enjoy a slice with a macchiato or cold brew or grab one to go. A second location is in Coconut Grove.

### 148 BUNNIECAKES

2322 NE 2nd Ave
Wynwood ③
+1 786 268 9790
*bunniecakes.com*

This adorable space caters to the vegan, the gluten-intolerant, the allergic and the health-conscious customer. Owner Mariana Cortez uses zero animal products in the baking of these cakes and cupcakes, but you wouldn't know it unless someone told you. Grab a half-dozen mini-cupcakes and a *café non-au lait* for a harm-free coffee break.

### 149 ALL DAY

1035 N Miami Ave
Wynwood ③
+1 305 699 3447
*alldaymia.com*

Pour over. Hot drip. Cold brew. Even cupping (as in, choose three coffees). This place knows its coffee. Pair any of them with pastries or breakfast dishes made in-house – the 'mostess' marshmallow fluff-stuffed cupcake is a fave, as is the *tres leches*-battered French toast with pecan butter, condensed milk and maple syrup.

### 150 CACHITO COFFEE AND BAKERY

251 71st St
North Beach ⑩
+1 786 973 8614
*cachitocoffee.com*

This appealing Latin-American coffee shop displays its heart on the surface of your cappuccino or latte. Designs change depending on which artisanal barrista is on duty, as do the daily, house-made *empanadas*, croissants, quiches, pies and tarts. Check the chalkboard for what's available, but do check in. Prices beat national chains, and so does atmosphere.

# 5 classic
# *VENTANITAS*
## (walk-up windows)

---

151 **THREE PALMS CUBAN CAFÉ**

**11500 Biscayne Blvd North Miami** ①
**+1 305 891 0046**
*threepalms restaurant.com*

Named for both a small Cuban town and the three employees that the owner started with, Three Palms always has a crowd. If you're a follower of reality television, you also already know that the Kardashian clan have discovered the authenticity of the *cafecito* here – if that means anything.

152 **VERSAILLES**

**3555 SW 8th St Little Havana** ⑦
**+1 305 444 0240**
*versailles restaurant.com*

Brush up on Cuban coffee vocab before you saunter up. You'll need to know the difference between a *cafecito* (with sugar) or a *cortadito* (with sugar and steamed milk). Then open your ears along with your lips. You'll hear the most incredible political and celebrity gossip – though hardly any of it's true.

153 **EL PUB RESTAURANT**

**1548 SW 8th St Little Havana** ⑦
**+1 305 642 9942**
*elpubrestaurant.com*

This long-running Cuban diner has made it into movies like *War Dogs* and become hip again. It becomes crowded at mealtimes, 3.05 pm (Miami's official coffee break!), and around midnight, after partiers on Calle Ocho want to sober up with a *colada*, a *cafecito* meant to be served like booze in shots.

### 154 EL EXQUISITO RESTAURANT

**1510 SW 8th St**
**Little Havana** ⑦
**+1 305 643 0227**
*elexquisitomiami.com*

Since 1974, this Cuban mainstay has been expanding and growing, adding partners and remodeling. But the *ventanita* has remained consistent, serving coffee, mamey or papaya *batidos* (smoothies), and other easy carry-out items. Award-winning, but it's still cost efficient.

### 155 MOLINA'S RANCH RESTAURANT

**4090 E 8th Ave**
**Hialeah** ⑯
**+1 305 693 4440**
*molinasranch*
*restaurant.com*

Here's the equation for a successful Cuban restaurant: family run + traditional recipes = dedicated patrons. Molina's is all that plus close to Miami International Airport; thus politicians and celebrities make it a first stop. Keep one eye on the *café Cubano,* the other on the clientele.

152 VERSAILLES

# *The 5 best*
# COCKTAIL
# THROWBACKS

---

### 156 PROHIBITION RESTAURANT AND SPEAKEASY

3404 N Miami Ave
Midtown ③
+1 305 438 9199
*prohibitionmiami.com*

It's always the 1920s in this classy joint, where the cocktails are updated takes on tradition. For instance, the French 75 uses Prosecco instead of Champagne and the Mojito adds fresh raspberries to its fresh mint. However, a globally oriented food menu ensures that you remember the actual century that you're in.

### 157 NANCY

2007 SW 8th St
Little Havana ⑦
+1 305 397 8971
*nancy305.com*

Named after a Colonial ship, the Revolutionary War-themed bar Nancy is run by renowned mixologists and features live music programming. Try the secret, off-menu drink, the 'VIP Captain's Call' (30 dollars): your favorite base spirits and flavor profiles custom crafted and served in a take-home octopus glass.

### 158 TAPAS Y TINTOS

448 Española Way
South Beach ⑫
+1 305 538 8272
*tapasytintos.com*

In business since 1982, this bar is a study in Spanish relics, with vintage costumes from matadors to futbol players to flamenco dancers decorating the walls. It's also a retrogressive homage to gin, with 18 different brands available.

## 159 SWEET LIBERTY DRINK & SUPPLY CO.

237-B 20th St
South Beach ⑫
+1 305 763 8217
*mysweetliberty.com*

This hometown hideout, founded by the late John Lermayer and longtime hospitality pros Dan Binkiewicz and David Martinez, combines discretion and erudition. The décor is classic neighborhood lounge; the cocktails and fare seriously inventive. From the 'Pana-maniac' to the 'Cauliflower Nachos!' the drinks and dishes endear from the get go.

## 160 FLOYD MIAMI

AT: CLUB SPACE
34 NE 11th St
Downtown ④
+1 786 618 9447
*floydmiami.com*

Located within the uber-popular Club Space, Floyd is a separate room where you can find musical artists, craft cocktails, and a distinctly speakeasy vibe. Dedicated to late nights and locals, Floyd hosts indie album drops, live band sets, DJ residencies in support of homegrown festivals, pioneering producers – and liquor promos.

157 NANCY

## 5 takes on
# TEA AND SYMPATHY

---

**161 SPECIALTEA LOUNGE & CAFÉ**
AT: COLUMBIA
SHOPPING PLAZA
**10766 SW 24th St**
**University Park** ⑮
**+1 305 554 8327**
*specialtealounge.com*

This lounge was the first eco-friendly tearoom in Miami. Today it continues to raise the level of earth consciousness as it serves more than 60 varieties of loose leaf teas, bobas and frozen teas, as well as natural, homemade sandwiches and desserts. Stay as long as you like. Free Wi-Fi.

**162 TEA & POETS**
AT: THE SHOPS
AT SUNSET PLACE
**5701 Sunset Drive**
**South Miami** ⑭
**+1 786 216 7201**

Need more energy? Fighting off a cold? At this quaint shop, the baristas will actually curate a tea blend according to your needs. In addition, the boutique is dedicated to creatives of all kinds, from sponsoring open mics to providing artisans a space to work on – and sell – their crafts.

## 163 COOL MONKEY

954 Normandy Drive
Normandy Isle
+1 305 763 8329

It's an interesting combo selling here, side by side: Bubble tea and gelato. The bubble tea, in flavors that range from green apple to jasmine, with molasses-infused bobas, is some of the best on the beach. As is the gelato. Even better, though, is when they're together: The bubble tea float reigns supreme.

## 164 SMALL TEA

205 Aragon Avenue
Coral Gables ⑨
+1 786 401 7189
smallteaco.com

A tribute to tea from all over the globe, this fetching shop ushers in patrons with gorgeous lighting and design, plus world music. All nine categories of teas are represented, from ayurvedic to oolong. Wonderfully aromatic. Wraps, paninis, breakfast items and sweets also available.

## 165 MY TEA BAR

AT: THE FALLS
8888 SW 136th St
Kendall ⑭
+1 786 732 7078
myteabar.net

Owner Mariedna Castro began her business as a pop-up. It soon progressed to its current brick-and-mortar status, serving its seasonal, anti-oxidant, loose-leaf teas to whoever wants or needs them. The minimalistic, pretty aesthetic, is just as soothing as the tea itself, and a perfect place to practice mindfulness and explore creativity.

# 5
# OLD-TIME DIVES

**166 MAC'S CLUB DEUCE**

222 14th St
South Beach ⑫
+1 305 531 6200
*macsclubdeuce.com*

Owned and run by Mac Klein from 1964 until his death at 101 in 2016, Miami's oldest bar has received a lot of attention since its earlier days. Still, you'll find no muddled cocktails or craft beer. Open 8 am to 5 am seven days a week, with 2-4-1 happy hour from 8 am to 7 pm.

**167 CORBETT'S SPORTS BAR & GRILL**

12721 S Dixie Hwy
Kendall ⑭
+1 305 238 0823

When you're in the mood for darts and 50 cent 'special grilled' wings, or a few bottles of beer and watching the basketball game on one of the 18 televisions, this is the place. Cheap drink specials and events like Ladies Night, Live Trivia and Karaoke. Lots of regulars tend to gawk at strangers.

**168 KEG SOUTH**

10417 S Dixie Hwy
Pinecrest ⑭
+1 305 284 9296

Open since the 1960s, this institution is famous for its burgers, its wings and, of course, its beer, as the name suggests. A very casual hangout for families, college students and sports fans. Not grimy, but good and dive-y.

169 **& HAPPY'S STORK LOUNGE LIQUOR STORE**
1872 79th St
North Bay Village ⑩
+1 305 865 3621

A mixture of native hipsters and old-timers frequent this basic lounge, which you could easily dismiss if you didn't know better. Great for basic drinks, domestic beers, a game on the television and cheerful drunks. Eat before you come unless you can subsist on nuts, chips and booze. Open from 11 am until 5 am.

170 **TED'S HIDEAWAY**
124 2nd St
South Beach ⑫
+1 305 532 9869

One of the few remaining places in South Beach where you don't have to pretend to be something you're not. Grab a few drinks and watch the game with friends or by yourself. Don't dress or wear cosmetics. Don't even shower. No one here cares. Open noon to 5 am daily.

166 **MAC'S CLUB DEUCE**

*5 joints for*

# DRINKING LIKE A LOCAL

---

### 171 THE ANDERSON

709 NE 79th St
MiMo District/
Upper East Side ②
+1 305 757 3368
*theandersonmiami.com*

Run by locals for locals, The Anderson is deceptive. It looks fairly nondescript from the road, but inside it's part tiki bar, part piano bar, and part shake-it-til-you-forget-how-old-you-are bar. This is where residents come before and after hurricanes, to celebrate victories large and small, and to beat back the work-week blues.

### 172 THE ABBEY BREWING CO.

1115 16th St
South Beach ⑬
+1 305 538 8110
*abbeybrewinginc.com*

If you're into The Grateful Dead, craft beer – and not much else – The Abbey is your place. Brewmaster Raymond Rigazio opened here in 1995; the locals who weren't models and celebs gave thanks; and the brewpub's history and future were written simultaneously. Open 1 pm to 5 am every day.

### 173 TAP 79 BREWS AND BURGERS

1071 NE 79th St
MiMo District/
Upper East Side ②
+1 305 381 0946
*tap79miami.com*

A square of a bar with a smattering of tables inside and out, this storefront attracts those in the know. Here's the intel: a smart menu with an emphasis on burgers; a global collection of wines and beer; and bartenders who recognize your face and pour you one as you walk in the door.

### 174 MAMA TRIED

207 NE 1st St
Downtown ④
*mamatriedmia.com*

If mama tried to keep us away from this bar, she failed. That's because locals can't resist this place, decorated like an episode of The Brady Bunch. The cocktails are trendy without being outlandish; the beer list is craft-y and local-ish; and there's a decent collection of wines by the glass, including some bubbly.

### 175 THE SPILLOVER BY LOKAL

2911 Grand Avenue
Coconut Grove ⑧
+1 305 456 5723
*spillovermiami.com*

For downtown dwellers and those in environs south, this ultra-cool concept, owned by Matt Kusher and company, is something different indeed. The fresh-caught seafood is one draw; the selection of cider and mead, which you can order solo or as flights, is another. Dine and drink inside, outside or at the bar.

173 TAP 79 BREWS AND BURGERS

## The 5 best
# WINE BARS

---

176 **GLASS AND VINE**
2820 McFarlane Rd
Coconut Grove ⑧
+1 305 200 5268
glassandvine.com

Under Miami native chef Giorgio Rapicavoli's direction, the menu here reflects the city's culture and regional farms, while the select wine list is sourced from all over to match such innovative dishes as pork 'steak frites' with charred scallion, fried yuca and *mojo* butter.

177 **BIG EASY WINEBAR & GRILL**
AT: BRICKELL CITY CENTRE
701 S Miami Avenue, #339a
Brickell ⑤
+1 786 814 5955
bigeasy.miami

Discovering South African cuisine and wine country flavors is most of the adventure here. The Angry Duck Curry and Nigerian Prawns with *peri-peri* sauce are perfect with owner (and legendary golf pro) Ernie Els' Big Easy Red Blend and Chenin Blanc.

178 **DOMAINE SOUVIOU WINE BAR BOUTIQUE**
5760 Sunset Drive
South Miami ⑭
+1 305 395 4060

The U.S. counterpart to a 15th-century chateau estate in Provence, which also produces excellent olive oil, this wine bar sells its own outstanding rosés and other Provençal wines. Pair them with escargots and puff pastry filled with Camembert. Linger inside or outside, or grab-and-go a lunch (if you must).

## 179 CHEF ADRIANNE'S VINEYARD RESTAURANT AND WINE BAR

11510 SW 147th Ave
Kendall ⑭
+1 305 408 8386
*chefadriannes.com*

Born to Cuban parents in Miami and a graduate of the Miami campus of Johnson & Wales, chef-owner and cookbook author Adrianne Calvo then trained in Napa Valley – which explains her wine bar reality. You can taste her hard-earned successes at this eponymous establishment, which she opened in 2007 to raves from label connoisseurs.

## 180 BARMELI69 GREEK BISTRO & WINE BAR

6927 Biscayne Blvd
MiMo District/
Upper East Side ②
+1 305 754 5558
*barmeli.com*

The big personality of owner Liza Meli is one reason that this place is so popular. The other is her taste in wines, a climate-friendly mix of southern European and Mediterranean. There's always something great being poured, or about to be opened, or waiting to be discovered.

176 GLASS AND VINE

# 5 *irresistible*

# JUICE BARS

---

### 181 RAW REPUBLIC MICRO JUICERY

20804 Biscayne Blvd
Aventura ①
+1 305 705 4226
*drinkrawrepublic.com*

This business model is owned and run by three first cousins who have all adopted the raw lifestyle, and who were born and raised in Aventura. In other words, they practise what they preach, where they preach it – that drinking unpasteurized, cold-pressed, organic juice is 'pear-adise'. Vegan bites, smoothies, and açai bowls also available.

### 182 GUARAPO ORGANIC JUICE BAR

171 NW 36th St
Wynwood ③
+1 786 452 8080
*guarapoorganic juicebar.com*

A multitude of cleanses, juice blends, smoothies and supplements are available to drink here. There's also a whole list of drinks for what ails you. Acne? Try the pineapple/carrot/apple. Hangover? Tomato/ginger/lemon/cane juice. From helping high blood pressure to easing your ulcers, Guarapo has got you covered. And for solids, there's quinoa bowls, sandwiches and wraps.

### 183 UNDER THE MANGO TREE

**737 5th St**
**South Beach** ⑫
**+1 786 558 5103**
*mangotreemiami.com*

This tiny shop is a powerhouse player in the juice world. That's because the product, as well as the intention, is pure. Owner Patricia Olesen has created some irresistible combinations, ranging from the 'Pink Dragon' with dragon fruit, banana and apple to hot and cold healthy teas and coffees like the 'Superfood Frap'.

### 184 MILK GONE NUTS

**18829 Biscayne Blvd**
**Aventura** ①
**+1 786 654 2973**
*milkgonenuts.com*

Not strictly juice, instead the liquids here are all plant-based milks, derived from tree and ground nuts, cocoa, greens, and some classic fruits. They're whipped into the most amazing shakes and smoothies, and frozen into creamy popsicles that are as pretty to look at as they are refreshing to eat.

### 185 JUICENSE

**2992 McFarlane Rd**
**Coconut Grove** ⑧
**+1 786 409 2371**
*juicense.com*

Created by specialists from New York, the juices here have up to five pounds of fresh fruit and vegetables pressed into each bottle. Whether you're looking to detox, cleanse, boost the immune system or simply enjoy some fresh vitamins and minerals, the liquids here – including nut milks and smoothies – are compliant and complete.

# *The 5 most significant*
# HAPPY HOURS

---

### 186 ZEST BAR & LOUNGE
AT: SOUTHEAST
FINANCIAL CENTER
**200 S Biscayne Blvd**
**Downtown** ④
**+1 305 374 9873**
*zestmiami.com*

The hours of tipsy delights don't get longer or better than this. Every weekday from 3 to 8 pm, chef-owners Cindy Hutson and Delius Shirley tempt the downtown workaholics who live in the sun but perhaps never really see it with craft beers, curated wines and cocktails.

### 187 TOSCANA DIVINO
AT: THE SHOPS AT
MARY BRICKELL VILLAGE
**900 S Miami Avenue**
**Brickell** ⑤
**+1 305 371 2767**
*toscanadivino.com*

Elegance is an oyster and a glass of Prosecco. Expedience is enjoying it at the walk-in bar during daily happy hour from 5.30 to 8 pm. And ecstasy is not being mobbed or mugged at this modern Italian restaurant, and carrying on a conversation in a modulated tone of voice.

### 188 VIA VERDI MIAMI
**6900 Biscayne Blvd**
**MiMo District/**
**Upper East Side** ②
**+1 786 610 3176**
*viaverdimiami.com*

This Italian restaurant and wine bar, run by twin chefs from Northern Italy, entices with an extra-long, exuberant happy hour. Because it lasts from 4 to 8 pm daily, it often overlaps with specials like '50% Off Dine-In Pasta Mondays' and '50% Off Bottle Wine List Wednesdays'. Feel 100% free to stay here all afternoon and evening.

### 189 BEAKER & GRAY

**2637 N Miami Ave**
**Wynwood** ③
**+1 305 699 2637**
*beakerandgray.com*

Happy hour isn't always about making yourself feel better, although this place is pretty darn good at that with drinks and food specials from 4 to 7 pm Monday to Friday. Beaker & Gray also likes to pay it forward with the 'Instant Karma' promotion. Every fourth week of the month, happy hour proceeds are donated to a charity.

### 190 KYU

**251 NW 25th St**
**Wynwood** ③
**+1 786 577 0150**
*kyumiami.com*

A former warehouse turned sustainable Asia barbecue joint, this well-liked place is often overbooked. Enter extended happy hour, Tuesday to Saturday (note: Saturday!) from 4.30 to 7.30 pm, when local J. Wakefield brews and the house's signature Wynwood Mule are marked down.

186 ZEST BAR & LOUNGE

EN AVANCE

# 70 PLACES
# TO SHOP

———

# The 5 best
# MALLS and
# SHOPPING DISTRICTS

## 191 BRICKELL CITY CENTRE

701 S Miami Ave
Brickell ⑤
+1 786 465 6533
brickellcitycentre.com

Anchored by an enormous Saks Fifth Avenue and a CMX movie complex – and connected to luxury hotel EAST, Miami – this four-level plaza is in another class entirely. Global brands, some with flagship U.S. stores, include Acqua Di Parma, Carmen Steffens and Michelle Lopriore. La Centrale – Italian Food Hall is a shopping experience for the palate.

## 192 LINCOLN ROAD MALL

Pedestrian road
running east-west
between 16th St
and 17th St
South Beach ⑫
lincolnroadmall.com

This mile-long promenade was designed by Miami Modern architect Morris Lapidus, with fountains, gardens and shade shelters, in the 1950s. Today it's home to homegrown stores like Books & Books, flagship shops for brands H&M and Zara, and sidewalk cafe after cafe that rub umbrella tables like elbows. The people watching is prime as beef.

### 193 WYNWOOD ARCADE

50 NW 24th St
Wynwood ③
+1 917 281 0330
*wynwoodarcade.com*

Wynwood Arcade distinguishes itself with one-and-only boutiques, and drinks and eats that aren't accessible anywhere else. These include Bonobos, Raphaella Booz, Patrizia Bozzi Designs and The Salty Donut. The building itself is a signature work of art, developed by a collaboration of architects and muralists.

### 194 MIAMI DESIGN DISTRICT

3841 NE 2nd Ave, #400
Miami Design
District ②
+1 305 722 7100
*miamidesigndistrict.net*

This 18-block district is a thriving mix of designer boutiques (Tom Ford, Loewe and Gucci), upscale restaurants, art installations and museums such as the Institute of Contemporary Art Miami. On Fridays, after you roam anchor Paradise Plaza, take in The Palm Court Performance Series, curated by Emilio Estefan.

### 195 BAL HARBOUR SHOPS

9700 Collins Ave
Bal Harbour ⑩
+1 305 866 0311
*balharbourshops.com*

Legendary. Groundbreaking. And exclusive. Those are the words that come to mind when Stanley Whitman's beautifully landscaped, open-air mall is mentioned. Opened in 1965 on the site of what used to be WWII barracks, Bal Harbour Shops is filled with every high-end store imaginable, from Balenciaga to Valentino, and bolstered by select restaurants.

# 5 of the best shops for
# TRENDY MIAMI CLOTHING

### 196 U-ROCK COUTURE

928 Ocean Dr
South Beach ⑬
+1 305 538 7625
urockcouture.com

Open since the mid-1990s on Ocean Drive, this rock culture-inspired clothing store – as implied by the double entendre name – offers stud-worthy duds and accessories. In many cases, those are literal studs or other embellishments. Get-you-noticed labels here for men and women include BB Simon, King Baby and Robin.

### 197 THE WEBSTER

1200 Collins Ave
South Beach ⑫
+1 305 674 7899
thewebster.us

Named for the 1935 art deco building in which the flagship store is housed, The Webster is an assemblage of unique designer fashion items for both men and women. Owner Laure Heriard Dubreuil debuted a second Webster in Bal Harbour in 2013.

### 198 IDA AND HARRY
AT: FONTAINEBLEAU
MIAMI BEACH

4441 Collins Ave
Miami Beach ⑪
+1 305 674 4781
fontainebleau.com

Named for the scions of the hotel's developers, this luxe boutique, located just off the lobby, offers items ranging from ripped jeans to embellished sneakers to cosmetics and cologne. The store carries more than 50 designer brands. Whether you're looking for John Varvatos or Valentino, Ida and Harry are here to help.

199 **120% LINO**
AT: SHOPS AT
MERRICK PARK
342 San Lorenzo
Avenue, #1025
Coral Gables ⑨
+1 305 774 1212
120percento.com

Although this resort-wear brand is actually Italian, it only has one store in Milan – and four in Miami. That's because it's flowing, natural fabrics are ideal for the region's hot, humid temperatures. If you didn't bring the right clothes, or want to augment the style of anyone in your family, visit *pronto*.

200 **GOLDEN BAR**
1570 Washington Ave
South Beach ⑫
+1 305 534 1220
golden.bar

This apparel-meets-accessories-greets-home design store has an independent location on South Beach, plus two locations in malls – one in Merrick Park and one in Dadeland. If that sounds confusing, no worries. What's not complicated is how easy the clothing is to love. For women, there's plenty of hippie-chic separates and sexy dresses; for men, cool dude concert-attending duds.

# 5 renowned
# MIAMI-BASED
# FASHION DESIGNERS

---

### 201 JULIAN CHANG

7246 Biscayne Blvd
MiMo District/
Upper East Side ②
+1 786 857 6934
julianchang
boutique.com

Julian Chang brings his designs to wearable life just north of a Trina Turk boutique. Known for his beautiful tailoring and structured, contemporary, playful looks, Peruvian native Chang has been a long-time favorite for locals for both off-the-rack outfits and custom cocktail pieces.

### 202 SIMONETT

88 NE 39th St
Miami Design
District ②
+1 786 801 0319
simonett.us

Born in Venezuela and raised in Miami, Simonett Pereira first opened in Wynwood, then in the Design District in 2019. The shop features a mixture of her own lines and curated collections of accessories and décor. Pereira also partners with like-minded businesses to host workshops and classes.

### 203 RENE RUIZ

18143 Biscayne Blvd
Aventura ①
+1 305 445 2352
reneruiz.net

Cuban-born Rene Ruiz debuted his first shop in Coral Gables, and quickly became a name to know for quality fabrics and sophisticated gowns. Now his chic designs are housed in an atelier in an Aventura shopping center, where customers range from brides and couture collectors to men seeking sophisticated, crafted clothing.

### 204 RAMONA LARUE BY ARIANNE

3400 N Miami Ave
Midtown ③
+1 305 456 8191
ramonalarue.com

These highly original separates and dresses are a fashionable tribute to designer Arianne Brown's mother, Mona, who taught the Coconut Grove native how to hand-paint silk. Every item begins life as actual art. Then the designs are transferred to flowing clothing, all manufactured in Miami, that sway to the tune of the body.

### 205 KATHE CUERVO
VARIOUS LOCATIONS

kathecuervo.
bigcartel.com

A team of jewelry designers devoted to minimalism, Kathe Cuervo works with copper, sterling silver, thread and beads. Many of their handwrought designs, forged in their home studio, are imbued with symbols and carry messages such as 'Trust your intuition.' Find in local stores such as Nomad Tribe, Green Monkey Yoga, L.Y.M. and Ziel Cycling Club.

201 JULIAN CHANG

## 5 *singular*
# SHOPS FOR WOMEN

---

### 206 VICKY VICTORIA

2401 Biscayne Blvd
Edgewater ③
+1 786 558 4910
vicky-victoria.com

Edgy, spot-on fashion – if you don't have it before you come to Miami, this is where you go to get it. You can outfit yourself from leopard print headband to pastel pink sock boots, or whatever's in style at the time. In Miami, urban glam's the game. Vicky Victoria, well, you get the point.

### 207 EN AVANCE

151 NE 141st St
Miami Design
District ②
+1 305 576 0056
enavance.co

Since 1993, this boutique for women, men, and the home has radiated elegance, sustainability and class. A pioneer in the Design District, moving here from Lincoln Road, owner Karen Quinones curates an outstanding collection of globally recognized designers. Outfit yourself from head to toe, or your home from ceiling to floor.

### 208 MVM MIAMI

2119 NW 2nd Ave
Wynwood ③
+1 954 606 0964
mvmmiami.com

Cutting-edge style from more than 40 designers, ranging from relative newcomers like Bailey 44 to fully established such as Derek Lam, hang in a long, narrow, polished format. Don't expect a deal, even on the sale rack, but do expect everything from beach gear to cocktail attire, plus frills and furbelows including lingerie and scarves.

### 209 BLUSH BOUTIQUE

1935 West Ave
South Beach ⑫
+1 305 531 3050
shopblush.com

This homegrown mini-chain of fashion-forward stores has offered locals and visitors alike the chance to dress 'Miami casual' since 1999. The average target is a Millennial, but mothers and daughters alike shop comfortably. The same team runs Market, boutiques featuring high-end basics and staples for the casual life, and Studio LX, which showcases upper-tier labels.

### 210 CATTIVA BOUTIQUE

257 Miracle Mile
Coral Gables ⑨
+1 305 774 1733
cattivaboutique.com

From jeans to jackets and swim suits to sweaters, this customer-oriented shop has it all. Unique but on-trend pieces display quality, and the shops – one in Coral Gables, the other in Doral – are craftily designed, with lovely displays of accessories and sitting areas for guests who are there for approval purposes only.

## *5 singular*
# SHOPS FOR MEN

---

### 211 **OFY**
AT: THE SHOPS AT
MARY BRICKELL VILLAGE
900 S Miami Ave
Brickell ⑤
+1 786 536 9194
ofyshop.com

Fans of Shameless will want to shop here, where OFY stands for… well, see the snapbacks and tees for illumination. Young and urban, the Brickell and Wynwood locations stock apparel, shoes, belts and more for the fearless fashion set. Brands include Stampd, Homework, Represent and Wings + Horns.

### 212 **BASICO WYNWOOD**
2347 NW 2nd Ave
Wynwood ③
+1 786 360 3688
shopbasico.com

The flagship store opened on South Beach selling mostly a single South American designer. Since then, the concept as well as the locations have expanded. Like its environment, the Wynwood site is a colorful hodge-podge of national and international labels. Outfit yourself from underwear to outerwear.

### 213 **BASE**
2215 NW 2nd Ave
Wynwood ③
+1 305 531 4982
baseworld.com

For many years a staple on Lincoln Road when South Beach was renovating, BASE moved its flagship store to Wynwood when that region showed regeneration. This should tell you one thing: BASE knows hip in clothing, books, gift items, cologne and other one-of-a-kind items.

### 214 LOWER EAST COAST

84 39th St
Miami Design
District ②
lowereastcoast.com

Part cool zine and book store, part indie clothing brand boutique, Lower East Coast reps lines with Miami street cred. In addition to their own brand, find Carhartt W.I.P., Days, Delicate Porcelain, Stray Rats, The Good Company, and more pushing sweats, tees, snapbacks, hoodies, keychains, and even the occasional skate deck.

### 215 SUPPLY & ADVISE

223 SE 1st St
Downtown ④
+1 305 960 2043
supplyandadvise.com

For the well-groomed guy whose office air-conditioning is set to 60 degrees, or who's visiting from colder climes. Clothing ranges from wool suits to office goods. Tired out by the large selection? Head upstairs to the on-site, antique barbershop for a soothing, restorative shave.

212 BASICO WYNWOOD

# 5 awesome
# ANTIQUE STORES

### 216 STONEAGE ANTIQUES

3236 NW S River Dr
West Little Havana ⑦
+1 305 633 5114
stoneage-antiques.com

Collecting and selling for more than half a century, this huge, riverside storefront specializes in nautical antiques, and often supplies props for TV and film sets. The inventory is vast, so try taking a virtual tour and then calling in your order. The business might be Stoneage but it's 21st-century tech savvy.

### 217 FLY BOUTIQUE

7235 Biscayne Blvd
MiMo District/
Upper East Side ②
flyboutiquevintage.com

Not just fly but super fly. Every available inch of this MiMo District spot is hung, stacked or positioned with some kind of treasure, with new pieces coming in every day. Racks of vintage clothing can yield luxury designer labels; furniture might be signed finds. If you love something, buy it, or someone else will.

### 218 WALT GRACE VINTAGE

300 NW 26th St
Wynwood ③
+1 786 483 8180
waltgracevintage.com

This gallery of electric guitars and vintage cars is certainly on the unusual side. It's for those who love the sound and look of these two things as much as founder Bill Goldstein, who named the place after a John Mayer song. Buy, sell or trade a guitar here, or drive away with a dream.

### 219 ANTIQUES & DESIGN MALL MIAMI

8650-90 Biscayne Blvd
MiMo District/
Upper East Side ②
+1 305 458 7134
antiquesdesign
miami.com

Not all of the tenants in the 20-showroom, mural-painted facility are antiques dealers. Some are designers; others deal in fine art. But many do specialize in art deco, mid-century and other 20th-century collectibles, including Deco Dreams, Castellarts and Michel Contessa Antiques. The mall also holds public events and participates in Art Basel.

### 220 ANDREA'S OLD TOWN ANTIQUES COLLECTIBLES

162 NW 29th St
Wynwood ③
+1 305 573 6210

The building's painted sign clues you in right away: It specializes in everything. Large furniture, rugs and lamps. Smaller pieces, including porcelain, crystal and china. Religious stuff. Memorabilia. And then there's this tidbit: 'Unusual items'. So think your grandmother's apartment plus hoarder. It could take days to happily explore.

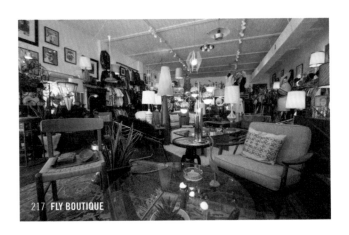

217 FLY BOUTIQUE

# The 5 most excellent
# VINTAGE AND THRIFT SHOPS

## 221 THE RABBIT HOLE

791 NE 125th St
North Miami ①
+1 305 892 0213
shoprabbithole.com

Specializing in clothing from the 1950–90s, this downtown North Miami boutique is great fun for the creative person who likes to mix vintage street style or party wear with modern-day items. Nothing is outrageously expensive, and there's a good variety of sizes. The owners also mix in some new pieces from up-and-coming artists and designers.

## 222 MIAMI TWICE

6562 SW 40th St
Ludlam ⑨
+1 305 666 0127
www.miamitwice.com

Opened in the 1980s, this store is an icon in the vintage fashion world. Visit for well-kempt pieces from the past whose time has returned, or for that perfect Halloween costume. Owners Mary Kyle Holle and Diane Kyle also know quality, so if collecting luxury labels from bygone eras is your gig, this is your place.

## 223 THE FASHIONISTA CONSIGNMENT BOUTIQUE

3135 Commodore Plaza
Coconut Grove ⑨
+1 305 443 4331
thefashionista
boutique.com

For all your top designer needs, frequent this mother-and-daughter store, in business for more than two decades. Vintage and lovingly used current stock from the world's most fashionable brands, from Balenciaga and Blumarine to Bottega Veneta and 7 For All Mankind, offer a palette for the stylish woman to paint a picture-perfect wardrobe.

## 224 THE LOTUS HOUSE THRIFT CHIC BOUTIQUE

2040 NW 7th Ave
Wynwood ③
+1 305 576 4112
lotushouse.org/
education

The mission here is admirable: The thrift shop outfits the homeless women and children who live at the Lotus House shelter; sells the overflowing surplus; and employs the women, allowing them to save money and learn skills for the real world. But come here also because the clothes, coming from wealthy, seasonal closet cleaners, rock.

## 225 DRAGONFLY THRIFT BOUTIQUE

3141 SW 8th St,
Suite A
West Flagler ⑦
+1 833 757 5327
dragonflythrift.org

Run by the Ladies Empowerment and Action Program (LEAP), this thrift store has a purpose: It provides education, mentorship, training, and post-release jobs to incarcerated women. Oh, and it also supplies some pretty cool vintage textiles, kitchenware, furniture, clothes, jewelry, books, and more, donated by affluent members of Miami society.

## 5 *happening*
# HOME DESIGN STORES

---

226 **CABLE URBAN MODERN**

3619 NW 2nd Avenue
Wynwood ③
+1 786 452 7880
cableisdesign.com

Cable offers a variety of services and consultancies. But the really cool stuff happens in the combination studio and showroom, where you can buy a banana doorstopper – because who doesn't need one of those? – or try out office items like the EarChair, a product that's designed with wings so wide they enclose you like a room.

227 **MRS. MANDOLIN**

4218 NE 2nd Ave
Miami Design
District ②
+1 786 420 5110
mrsmandolin.com

An extension of the beloved Miami restaurant, Mandolin Aegean Bistro, this boutique bills itself as a lifestyle shop – and that's exactly what it provides. From the perfect artisanal dishware to the colorful pillows that brighten your interior, Mrs. Mandolin knows exactly what home goods will bring life to the party.

## 228 BHOOM SHANTI

5050 Biscayne Blvd,
#100
MiMo District/
Upper East Side ②
+1 305 758 8282
bhoomshanti.com

For colorful textiles, pillows, footstools, statues and compact, inlaid tables from the Indian subcontinent, there's Bhoom Shanti, which translated literally from Hindi means 'Earth Peace'. Certainly a boutique for our times, the flagship store on Biscayne also sells incense, jewelry and authentic men's and women's clothing, as does a second location in South Miami.

## 229 NISI B HOME

39 NE 39th St
Miami Design
District ②
+1 305 573 1939
nisibhome.com

Founder Nisi Berryman has a fondness for artisan producers and opulence, a contradiction that is not at all at irreconcilable. Step into the showroom to see how she puts together singular classic or vintage pieces with contemporary glass or metallic vases, trays, and candlesticks to striking effect. You'll want to try this at home.

## 230 GLOTTMAN

2213 NW 2nd Ave
Wynwood ③
+1 305 438 3711
glottman.com

Whether you're looking for big installations (furniture, lighting systems, storage, flooring) or little *objets d'art* and home items, you're going to find a modern, eclectic assortment at architect Oscar Glottman's place. Many will prove irresistible, such as the skateboard mirror, or the etched metal bookmarks shaped like a pointing finger, a fountain pen or a quill.

## The 5 nicest boutiques for
# UNUSUAL GIFTS

231 **INIVA MIAMI**

5010 NE 2nd Ave,
#202
MiMo District/
Upper East Side ②
+1 786 451 0810
inivaboutiques.com

Stylist Sandra Bellon and designer Sophie Pozmentier run this concept store dedicated to African artists and artisans from countries including Kenya, Tanzania and Senegal. Sibling to two boutiques in Gabon and Burkina Faso, the INIVA Miami location stocks photography, handmade bronze jewelry, juju hats, limited edition masks, eco-friendly wax print clothing and more.

232 **COCO BELLA**

305 Alcazar Ave
Coral Gables ⑨
+1 305 444 1334
cocobellamiami.com

Sometimes you find the gift you've been looking for (like presents for bridesmaids/groomsmen, or a trinket for a beloved teacher, or something for that person who collects holiday paraphernalia) when you're not looking for it. Coco Bella houses so many cute items that you leave with an armful of them.

### 233 LA ISLA

1561 SW 8th St
Little Havana ⑦
+1 786 317 3051
laislausa.com

One-third gallery, one-third gift shop and one-third artist hangout, La Isla is run by freelance textile designer, Eliott Prada. The products range from a line of T-shirts and mugs with screens of Frida Kahlo to original artwork and jewelry to custom fedoras. Make this a stop on your Calle Ocho tour.

### 234 EFFUSION GALLERY

1130 Ocean Dr
South Beach ⑫
+1 305 538 3558
effusiongallery.com

Call it 'Pop-Mod Deco'. The 40 artists represented here, whose work represents a range of prices, is a melting pot of Miami's primary influences. Mixed media pieces have elements of pop culture, mid-century modern, art deco and more. Browse through the flagship store on South Beach or its sibling in Bayside Marketplace.

### 235 FRANGIPANI

2516 NW 2nd Ave
Wynwood ③
+1 305 573 1480
frangipanimiami.com

Kids. If you've got 'em, check out the adorable selection, from flamingo necklaces to Keith Haring placemats, that this whimsical store stocks. The quirkiness doesn't end with the children, though – the women's, men's and home sections all reflect the eye of owner Jennifer Frehling, who selects products for the joy they'll bring.

# 5 awesome stores for
## SPORTS

---

**236 SOCCER LOCKER**

9601 S Dixie Hwy
Pinecrest ⑭
+1 305 670 9100
*soccerlocker.com*

The international popularity of futbol is reflected in Miami's diverse population. Soccer Locker caters to that obsession with a significant selection of footwear, apparel and equipment. The employees are also happy to share which bars are soccer friendly, where to play a pick-up match, and how to find a club or camp.

**237 MIAMI NAUTIQUE INTERNATIONAL**

3828 NW 2nd Ave
Wynwood ③
+1 305 438 9464
*miamiskinautiques.com*

For wakeboards and water skis, look no further. This long-running business supplies the equipment you need, plus the wetsuits and life vests so that you can not only slalom the waves, but survive them, too. Yep, even in free-styling Miami, precautions are important, allow Nautique to kit you out.

## 238 HIGH FIVE SKATESHOP

315 Lincoln Road
South Beach ⑫
+1 305 531 6112
highfivesk8.com

Need a deck? Looking for wheels? Have a hankering for helmets and pads? Whatever your needs, High Five is ready to lend a hand. The store stocks dozens of brands, along with a fashionable selection of skate apparel and videos of professionals showing off their tricks.

## 239 THE SUPERIOR BIKE SHOP

776 NW 21st Terrace
Allapattah ③
+1 305 504 1362
thesuperiorbikeshop.com

High-end and technology-driven, The Superior lives up to its moniker by offering three elite brands, produced explicitly for maneuvering in urban environments: Schindelhauer, Fabike and 8bar. Of course, you'll pay between 2000 to 7000 dollars for the privilege of owning one. But it costs nothing to look.

## 240 PELÉ SOCCER

810 Lincoln Road
South Beach ⑫
+1 786 359 4147
pelesoccer.com

Literally fun and games, this Brazilian soccer player's superstore is covered with turf so that players can test their cleats and balls before buying. It also plans to hold watch parties on custom-built bleachers in the 7000-square-foot store, which stocks jerseys from more than 150 national and international teams.

## *The 5 best*
# FLEA MARKETS

241 **THE OPA LOCKA HIALEAH FLEA MARKET**

12691 NW 42 Ave
Opa-Locka ①
+1 305 688 0500
*opalockahialeah fleamarket.com*

This market offers legit stats: Open for more than 40 years, seven days per week. It covers more than 55 acres. You can visit more than 500 stores. And when you do, you'll be joining 15.000+ visitors weekly. No medals if you see it all at once, but it will be impressive nevertheless.

242 **REDLAND MARKET VILLAGE**

24420 S Dixie Hwy
Redland ⑬⑭
+1 305 257 4335
*redlandmarket village.com*

Since 1987, this sprawling market – which includes a generous farmers' market – has been enticing visitors to the Redland and Homestead farming regions. In fact, it started with vegetables, and has since expanded over 27 acres to include all sorts of goods, including antiques, leather (especially cowboy boots), tools, toys, and jewelry. Thursday-Sunday.

### 243 TROPICANA FLEA MARKET

2951 NW 36th St
Allapattah ③
+1 305 316 7594
*tropicana
fleamarket.com*

Tropicana is one of Miami's longest-running fleas. It's also one of the largest, with 200 vendors selling everything from pet products to auto materials, A food court, farmers' market, and plenty of shoes, clothing and jewelry merchants are enough to keep you occupied for hours – if not all day. Friday-Sunday.

### 244 THRIFTER MARKET
#### AT: THE WYNWOOD MARKETPLACE

2250 NW 2nd Ave
Wynwood ③
+1 305 239 8833
*thrifter.cool*

Located at The Wynwood Marketplace, this arts-and-crafts flea featuring local makers suits the neighborhood. You never know who will be selling what, but vintage or handmade clothing, art, jewelry, and homemade foodstuffs are a good rule of thumb. The Deck cocktail bar, food trucks and live music add to the festivities. Thursday-Sunday.

### 245 ART DECO ARTISAN MARKET
#### AT: LUMMUS PARK

Ocean Drive at
14th Place
South Beach ⑫
+1 305 906 1287
*metroflea.miami*

Operated by Metroflea Miami and lined up under orderly tents, this beachside flea offers artisanal and upcycled jewelry and clothing, crafts, foodstuffs, and more. It's a great pit stop to or on the way back from the beach when you're already carrying a tote for your purchases, and don't need extra bags.

## 5 bodegas and markets to buy
# INTERNATIONAL NECESSITIES

---

**246 MARKY'S**

687 NE 79th St
MiMo District/
Upper East Side ②
+1 305 758 9288
markys.com

Go ahead – covet the caviar. And the foie gras. And the truffles. The imported goods beckon. But the reality is, you don't have to just browse. For the most part, prices are no higher than at gourmet grocery chains, and there are delicacies that you can't find anywhere else.

**247 SENTIR CUBANO**

3100 SW 8th St
Little Havana ⑦
+1 305 644 8870
cubanfoodmarket.com

The equivalent of a general store, this market stocks everything from bread for *medianoche* sandwiches to several varieties of finely ground coffee for extra-strength *cortaditos*. Even more helpful is that you can buy the actual, authentic appliances to make the food and drink, too.

**248 PUBLIX SABOR**

Miami and
Hialeah ⑯
publix.com/pages/
publix-sabor

Just about every Miamian shops at a Publix for groceries. But Publix Sabor is pretty special. Only a few of these pan-Latin versions exist for the sole purpose of providing goods to the Hispanic community. They're a great way to familiarize yourself with the real flavor of the city.

### 249 EUROPEAN DELIGHTS MARKET & DELI

17080 Collins Ave
Sunny Isles Beach ①
+1 305 974 0084

This grocery and deli is located in an area of Miami heavily populated by Russians and Eastern Europeans, so don't be surprised to hear Russian. This is also the reason why you can get rich sour cream, pickled herring, smoked salmon, eggplant and pepper spreads, imported sweets, and house-made pastries, among other delicacies.

### 250 LA BODEGA – PERUVIAN RESTAURANT & STORE

13774 SW 88th St
Kendall ⑭
+1 305 386 8836

You might want to first dine on octopus in olive sauce, spoonfuls of ceviche or any of the numerous fish and seafood dishes first. Then visit the shelves at the back of the establishment, where you can purchase sauces, packaged mixes and Peruvian products to continue the experience at home.

249 LAURENZO'S ITALIAN CENTER

## The 5 best
# MIAMI SOUVENIRS

### 251 MIAMI HEAT JERSEY
AT: AMERICAN
AIRLINES ARENA
601 Biscayne Blvd
Downtown ④
+1 786 777 1000
aaarena.com

Like any professional team, the Miami Heat has its ups and downs. But the last decade has seen more of those ups, and even its downs don't seem so low. Celebrate the heart this team displays, no matter who gets traded, by purchasing a jersey at a game. It'll make you feel warm all over.

### 252 BOTTLE OF MIAMI'S ONLY CITY-DISTILLED RUM
AT: MIAMI CLUB RUM
6468 NW 77th Court
Miami Springs ⑮
+1 844 642 2582
miamiclubrum.com

The city's first distillery offers hourly tours of its facility; these include tastings of the rum, made with local Florida ingredients. Buy a bottle to bring home (but only if you're checking your bags). The next time you make a mojito, you'll practically hear the rumba in your glass.

### 253 FEDORAS
AT: HATS & HATS BY
PUERTO FINO HATS
1836 NE 163rd St
North Miami Beach ①
+1 305 944 8202
hatsandhats.net

You can never go wrong in Miami wearing a fedora. Timeless and trendless, it's ideal for anybody, regardless of age or gender. Find the perfect one to take home – material, color, shape of crown and brim – at this establishment, which has 2000-square-feet of headgear available.

### 254 UNIVERSITY OF MIAMI HURRICANES GEAR

AT: UNIVERSITY OF MIAMI

1306 Stanford Drive
Coral Gables ⑨
+1 305 284 4101
bkstr.com/miamistore/home/en

College sports fans know how mighty the Division I Hurricanes can be. Stop into the bookstore for a commemorative hoodie before watching a home baseball game at 'The U's' Alex Rodriguez Park at Mark Light Field or a basketball game at the Watsco Center. (Note: Football games are played off campus at Hard Rock Stadium.)

### 255 TROPICAL HOT SAUCE

AT: LA ESQUINA DEL LECHÓN

8601 NW 58th St,
#101
Doral ⑯
+1 305 640 3041
esquinalechon.com

As the name suggests, this popular Latin restaurant specializes in pig products. To go with its grilled, fried and roasted pork dishes, it serves – and sells – bottles of Garlic Serrano, Caribbean Lime, Red Habanero and Habanero Mango hot sauces. Buy one or all four with a carrier and take Miami's heat with you.

253 FEDORAS

# 5

# UNEXPECTED OUTLETS

256 **DOLPHIN MALL**

11401 NW 12th St
Sweetwater ⑮
+1 305 365 7446
*shopdolphinmall.com*

It's hard not to feel your heart racing. With more than 240 retailers in one huge setting – many value oriented – you almost don't know where to go first. Here are some favorites: Banana Republic Factory Store. Bloomingdales's – The Outlet Store. Vans Outlet. ALDO Outlet. Neiman Marcus Last Call. Try to stay calm.

257 **GUESS FACTORY**
AT: THE SHOPS
AT MIDTOWN MIAMI

3252 NE 1st Ave, #100
Midtown ③
+1 786 453 0336
*stores.guess.com*

In between Wynwood and Miami Design District, both of which house fairly pricey boutiques, there's Midtown. And in Midtown, there's the outlet for Guess, where you can get a terrific selection of men's and women's clothing and accessories – including sunglasses, shoes, jewelry, watches, wallets and handbags – at great prices.

## 258 SKECHERS FACTORY OUTLET
### AT: MIAMI GATEWAY
805 NW 167th St
North Miami Beach ①
+1 305 627 0535
local.skechers.com

Cute, comfortable, colorful – you can find lots of ways to describe these casual, athletic shoes. But at this factory outlet store, where they stock a healthy selection of both adult and kid sizes, the best one is affordable. Check the online site for electronic coupons, too.

## 259 GAP OUTLET
### AT: KENDALL VILLAGE CENTER
8705 SW 124th Ave
Kendall ⑭
+1 305 412 1139
gap.com

When you need basic tees, jeans, chinos, button-downs, cardigans and swimwear, nothing beats the GAP – except for the GAP Outlet store. There, you can find all of the aforementioned at a fraction of the original prices. And often a storewide sale is taking place, making everything that much more irresistible.

## 260 G & P FACTORY OUTLET
559 NW 28th St
Wynwood ③
+1 305 358 4650

Pamper your skin like you don't care – about the price, that is. Here you can indulge in spa-worthy serums, lotions, body butters and creams for both genders. A large selection of perfumes and colognes are exactly what you need to smell like a superstar and still stay within your means.

OFFICE

THE VAGABOND MOTEL

# 20 BUILDINGS TO ADMIRE

---

## The 5 most amazing
# ART DECO
# RENOVATIONS

---

### 261 THE COLONY THEATRE

1040 Lincoln Road
South Beach ⑫
+1 800 211 1414
colonymb.org

With its unmistakable movie marquee and streamlined, geometric architecture rising behind it, The Colony is one of the last original buildings on Lincoln Road. It debuted as Paramount Pictures in 1938 and underwent a 6,5-million-dollar restoration 80 years later. Cherish every step on those priceless terrazzo floors.

### 262 HOTEL BREAKWATER

940 Ocean Drive
South Beach ⑫
+1 305 532 2362
breakwater
southbeach.com

Architect Anton Skislewicz designed this emblematic structure in 1936. Formerly pastel, it is now a magnificent blue-and-orange façade, with the enormous neon sign that spells out the name of the hotel fronting the parapet, and vertical lines shooting out from the sides of the frieze.

### 263 MIAMI CITY HALL

3500 Pan American Drive
Coconut Grove ⑧
+1 305 250 5400
miamigov.com/home

This was Pan American Airlines' airport for the famous flying seaplanes. The 1934 building featured interior murals and a stunning, curved canopy. Many of the art deco elements were hidden with a bland redo in 1954 when it became City Hall, but it was restored to its former self in 2003.

261 THE COLONY THEATRE

## 264 CADILLAC HOTEL & BEACH CLUB

3925 Collins Avenue
Miami Beach ⑪
+1 305 538 3373
hotelcadillac
miamibeach.com

Now owned by Marriott, this hotel really was whimsically designed to resemble a car, with plenty of chrome trim, a canopy shaped like a car hood and a sign lighted in what could be headlights. Constructed in 1940 from a Roy France design, it's the tallest art deco building, offering unparalleled access of the Atlantic.

## 265 COLONY HOTEL

736 Ocean Drive
South Beach ⑫
+1 305 673 0088
colonymiami.com

This art deco restoration has dominated every skyline since South Beach reinvented itself. The bright blue neon signage, the flat roof with more neon enlivening it, the tri-level division. It's earned its place in the postcards.

# 5 *stunning*
# MEDITERRANEAN REVIVAL BUILDINGS

## 266 CORAL GABLES CITY HALL

405 Biltmore Way
Coral Gables ⑨
+1 305 446 6800
*coralgables-fl.gov*

Given that this planned community site was finished in 1928, at the height of the architectural trend, it makes sense to visit it for those notable features: stuccoed walls, roof tiles, clock tower and, most strikingly, its frontal Corinthian colonnade. Designed by Phineas Paist and Harold Steward, it was created from limestone quarried nearby.

## 267 HOTEL ST. MICHEL

162 Alcazar Avenue
Coral Gables ⑨
+1 305 444 1666
*hotelstmichel.com*

Part of George Merrick's Spanish-Mediterranean 'City Beautiful', this lodging was built in 1926 and originally called the Sevilla Hotel. Today the boutique property, with its stucco, carved stonework, wrought iron detailing and balconies, is still a lovely place to stay. Already have a place? Dine at the elegant Zucca Ristorante and explore the property.

## 268 VIZCAYA VILLAGE
ACROSS: VIZCAYA
MUSEUM & GARDENS
3251 S Miami Avenue
Coconut Grove ⑧
+1 305 250 9133
vizcaya.org/vizcaya-
village.asp

Vizcaya, James Deering's bayfront mansion, is a Mediterranean Revival masterpiece of its own. The Vizcaya Village, where his staff lived and worked, is a newly restored part of the estate. These 11 buildings, from 1916, are now used for cultural/arts programming, horticulture and native conservation, and urban farming.

## 269 OLYMPIA THEATER
174 E Flagler St
Downtown ④
+1 305 374 2444
olympiatheater.org

A stunning piece of architecture in downtown Miami, the Olympia began life as a silent movie theater in 1926, and later became respected for both Vaudeville and air-conditioning. It's also been known, at various points of restoration, for its interior turrets and towers, a ceiling painted like a night sky, balconies and a courtyard.

## 270 THE VILLA CASA CASUARINA
1116 Ocean Drive
South Beach ⑫
+1 786 485 2200
vmmiamibeach.com

This over-the-top site was constructed in 1930 by adventurous architect Alden Freeman, who modeled the home after the Alcazar de Colon, even using a brick from it that he brought back. It was purchased by Gianni Versace in 1992, who renovated and added more gilded features; Casa Casuarina was also where he was tragically killed.

# 5 *Miami modern*
# MOTELS

---

**271 SINBAD MOTEL MIAMI**

6150 Biscayne Blvd
MiMo District/
Upper East Side ②
+1 305 751 3110

Designed by Tony Sherman to resemble a ship – because the bay was visible then from the property – this blocky 1953 motel, complete with brise-soleils and winged overhangs, was named after Sinbad the Sailor. Its instantly recognizable neon signs, which remain today, are featured in the 1995 movie *Miami Rhapsody*.

**272 NEW YORKER BOUTIQUE HOTEL**

6500 Biscayne Blvd
MiMo District/
Upper East Side ②
+1 305 759 5823
*newyorker
boutiquehotel.us*

Showcasing the neon signs and angular façade, this hotel is in the hands of the family who have owned it since the 1980s. Renovated (with lots of flamingo décor) in 2009 to keep up with the changing MiMo District landscape, they solicit a clientele interested in quiet quality and offer a funky, outdoor happy hour in the courtyard.

**273 SHALIMAR MOTEL**

6200 Biscayne Blvd
MiMo District/
Upper East Side ②
+1 305 751 0345
*shalimarmotel.com*

Architect Edwin Reeder designed this motel in 1951, and it stood apiece with the ramshackle others until a complete redo was accomplished in 2013. Streamlined with community balconies and MiMo accents – including the signature neon sign – it offers clean, reasonably priced lodging.

274 THE VAGABOND HOTEL

## 274 THE VAGABOND HOTEL

7301 Biscayne Blvd
MiMo District/
Upper East Side ②
+1 305 400 8420
*thevagabondhotel.com*

With its futuristic asymmetry and angularity, The Vagabond was a vision of Miami Modern. Designed in 1953 by Robert Swartburg, it was a magnet motel/lounge for the Rat Pack. Today it has been thoroughly reinvented and modernized, with a chic pool scene, high-end eatery and more.

## 275 BISCAYNE INN

6730 Biscayne Blvd
MiMo District/
Upper East Side ②
+1 305 756 0366
(resto)

While this property has the history and elements of the architecture, renting a room isn't possible, as the property is closed at the moment. Instead, go here to admire the neon sign, complete with a palm tree for an 'I' in 'Inn', and dine at Danny Serfer's Blue Collar restaurant, serving some of the best comfort food in Miami.

# 5 of the most
# ICONIC MIAMI
# MASTERPIECES

### 276 FREEDOM TOWER

AT: MIAMI DADE COLLEGE

600 Biscayne Blvd
Downtown ④
+1 305 237 7700
*mdcmoad.org/
freedom-tower*

One of the most culturally meaningful landmarks in the city, this model of Seville's Giralda Cathedral Bell Tower was built in 1925. Its history includes being used to process Cuban exiles from 1962 to 1974 – thus its nickname. It originally housed The Miami News, and now hosts the MDC Museum of Art + Design.

### 277 FONTAINEBLEAU MIAMI BEACH

4441 Collins Avenue
Miami Beach ⑪
+1 800 548 8886
*fontainebleau.com*

Perhaps the most compelling example of futuristic MiMo architecture, the 'curvilinear' Fontainebleau was designed by legendary architect Morris Lapidus in 1954. As glamorous now as it was then, the 22-acre beachfront property is an attraction for global celebrities, professional athletes and cognoscenti.

### 278 THE BASS

2100 Collins Avenue
South Beach ⑫
+1 305 673 7530
*thebass.org*

Designed by Russell Pancoast in the 1930s, this unique art deco contemporary art museum was first a public library. In 2017, it reopened with a 12 million-dollar expansion of its exhibition and program spaces, cafe and a museum store, while still making use of its historic galleries.

### 279 HIALEAH PARK RACING & CASINO

100 E 32nd St
Hialeah ⑯
+1 305 885 8000
*hialeahparkcasino.com*

Glitzy and lavish with balustrades and curving staircases, this 1920s Mediterranean Revival structure, set on 200 acres, is as captivating as it is entertaining. It's the only race course listed on the National Register of Historic Places and, because of its flock of resident flamingos, originally brought over from Cuba, as an Audubon Bird Sanctuary.

### 280 MIAMI TOWER

100 SE 2nd St
Downtown ④
*miamitower.net*

This signature 47-story skyscraper lights up in different colors or patterns to suit the occasion, be it a holiday, a season or even a Dolphins game. A graduating, three-tiered glass spire that rises above a 10-story parking garage, this office building was originally built for CenTrust Bank.

276 **FREEDOM TOWER**

# 40 PLACES
# TO DISCOVER
# MIAMI

## *5 awesome*
# VIEWS OF DOWNTOWN

---

### 281 THE RUSTY PELICAN

**3201 Rickenbacker
Causeway
Virginia Key** ⑥
**+1 305 361 3818**
*therustypelican.com*

Soaring sea birds. Boats whose sails fly just as high. And an encapsulated view of downtown Miami. That's what you see when you perch at The Rusty Pelican, which underwent a 7 million-dollar renovation in 2011 and later unveiled a wine menu featuring more than 300 bottles. Sip, stare and sink into bliss.

### 282 SUGAR

AT: EAST, MIAMI
**788 Brickell Plaza
Brickell** ⑤
**+1 786 805 4655**
*east-miami.com*

This rooftop lounge and garden puts the 'scene' in scenic. Crowning the 40th floor, it features 360-degree views of the downtown region and the water – although you'll have to tear yourself away from the lush landscaping and Asian tapas in order to take it all in.

### 283 WET DECK LOUNGE

AT: W MIAMI
**485 Brickell Avenue
Brickell** ⑤
**+1 305 503 4417**
*wmiamihotel.com/
miami-nightclub*

Be prepared to feel high. This gorgeously designed lounge, located on the 50th floor of the hotel, is meant to stimulate every one of the senses. But if you love a great view, this is the place to find it, because you can see practically all of downtown and the bay from here.

### 284 MATHESON HAMMOCK PARK

9610 Old Cutler Road
Coral Gables ⑨
+1 305 665 5475
miamidade.gov/parks/
matheson-hammock.asp

Sit on the family-friendly beach and watch your little ones wade in the atoll pool. Behind them, kite boarders soar against the pinks and golds of late-afternoon sun, striking off the skyscrapers of distant downtown Miami. You couldn't ask for better Instagram snaps.

### 285 VENETIAN CAUSEWAY

A series of 12
bridges (10 fixed,
2 bascule) connecting
11 islands from
Downtown to
South Beach ③⑫
miamidade.gov/parks/
venetian.asp

The sights from these low-rising bridges, located northeast of downtown, are outstanding during the day. But thanks to the architects who built Miami and their penchant for adding neon hues to various skyscrapers, some of the coolest illuminations of the scene are at night.

285 VENETIAN CAUSEWAY

# The 5 nicest
# WATER VIEWS

---

### 286 NAUTILUS CABANA CLUB

1825 Collins Avenue
South Beach ⑫
+1 786 483 2650
*nautiluscabana
club.com*

A lovely beachside hotel, Nautilus offers this stunner of a beach club that includes permanent cabanas, a wooden deck and absolutely lush, tropical landscaping that leads to the long, wide Atlantic stretching out like a blanket. Still, the best water view may be of the unique, long-step, saltwater pool on the premises.

### 287 PALMEIRAS BEACH CLUB AT GROVE ISLE

4 Grove Isle Drive
Grove Isle ⑧
+1 305 858 8300
*palmeirasbeachclub.com*

The waves of Biscayne Bay literally lap at your feet while you dine on fresh fish, down a Champagne cocktail, or chill on a chaise lounge under an umbrella at this chic establishment. So there's just no arguing: This beach club is tops when it comes to peering at the peerless sea that surrounds Miami.

### 288 BAYSIDE MARKETPLACE

401 Biscayne Blvd
Downtown ④
*baysidemarketplace.com*

Bayside is a busy place for commerce and entertainment. But its name clues you into its location: It's built next to Biscayne Bay. You can walk the paths and watch the animated party boats take off from the marina, or sit on the benches, cast your eyes further toward the horizon and meditate.

### 289 THE KAMPONG

4013 S Douglas Road
Coconut Grove ⑧
+1 305 442 7169
ntbg.org/gardens/
kampong

Listed on the National Register of Historic Places, The Kampong is an incredible collection of historic fruit cultivars and flowering trees, many of them from Southeast Asia. The tropical oasis leads down to sparkling panoramas of Biscayne Bay.

### 290 JULIA TUTTLE CAUSEWAY/ INTERSTATE 195

4,4 miles
connecting I-95
to Miami Beach,
Edgewater to
Miami Beach ③⑪

Miami is famous for being flat as paper, but the Julia Tuttle rises above – literally. As one of the causeways connecting the mainland to the beaches, it can almost be called a hill. At the crest, drivers can see the Atlantic, dotted with mangrove islands and water craft, extending on both sides.

288 BAYSIDE MARKETPLACE

# 5 great
# NEIGHBORHOODS

---

### 291 ESPAÑOLA WAY HISTORIC DISTRICT
**South Beach** ⑫

This historic, pedestrian-only boulevard was originally designed as an artists' colony in the 1920s and frequented by notables in the field such as Kenny Scharf, Desi Arnaz, Miralda and Craig Coleman. It was redeveloped and relaunched in 2017 by Craig Robins, who modeled the design after Barcelona's Las Ramblas.

### 292 BRICKELL
**Brickell Avenue and associated streets, Downtown Miami Brickell** ⑤

The bustling, beating heart of the downtown business district, Brickell Avenue and its connecting side streets – commonly shortened to simply 'Brickell' – is a cosmopolitan collection of condominiums, luxury hotels, restaurants, bars and assorted retail establishments.

### 293 BIRD ROAD ART DISTRICT
**7259 SW 48th St Olympia Heights** ⑮
**+1 305 467 6819**
*thebirdroad artwalk.com*

Previously, this industrial tract, located by railroad tracks, was filled with warehouses. Artists began converting those buildings into studios in the 1980s. The District now includes galleries, art schools, and stages for live theater, music, and spoken word performances.

## 294 LITTLE HAITI

The southern border North (NW/NE) 54th St, west to Interstate 95 and north along the Miami city boundary on North (NW/NE) 80th St; East (NE) 2nd and 4th Avenues

Home to the many immigrants from Haiti and other Caribbean islands, Little Haiti (and its neighbor, Little River) is also an up-and-coming arts-and-entertainment district. Galleries, boutiques and restaurants are moving in next door to traditional Caribbean eateries and shops. It's a colorful and evocative blend that locals hope will keep its character as it develops.

## 295 MIMO BISCAYNE BLVD HISTORIC DISTRICT

MIMO BISCAYNE ASSOCIATION
8101 Biscayne Blvd, #309-310
MiMo District/ Upper East Side ②
+1 786 391 3993
*mimoboulevard.org*

Short for Miami Modern, the MiMo District is also known as the Upper East Side. It encompasses a swatch of Biscayne Boulevard and the neighborhoods of Morningside and Shorecrest, which contain wonderful examples of mid-century modern architecture. Once a desolate strip, today the MiMo District is a thriving, resurgent community.

291 ESPAÑOLA WAY HISTORIC DISTRICT

# *The 5 most beautiful*
# BOTANIC GARDENS

---

**296 THE JOHN C. GIFFORD ARBORETUM**

AT: 231 COX SCIENCE CENTER

1301 Memorial Drive
University of Miami
Coral Gables ⑨
+1 305 284 1302
*bio.miami.edu/arboretum*

Take your time strolling through and relaxing in this teaching and research facility. These 500 or so species of tropical plants and trees, originally collected and nurtured in 1947, have survived multiple hurricanes and other catastrophes. Its University of Miami campus scientist caretakers, who use it for educational purposes, welcome visitors for self-guided tours.

**297 PINECREST GARDENS**

11000 Red Road
Pinecrest ⑭
+1 305 669 6990
*pinecrestgardens.org*

Pinecrest Gardens takes its plants pretty seriously, offering horticulture workshops for those who not only admire the collections here but also want to work with them elsewhere. Still, this 'cultural arts park' also features tons of entertainment: concerts, theater and dance performances, holiday-themed festivals such as 'Howl-O-Ween', family movie nights and Sunday farmers' markets.

297 PINECREST GARDENS

## 298 CASTELLOW HAMMOCK PRESERVE & NATURE CENTER

22301 SW 162nd Ave
Redland ⑬⑭
+1 305 242 7688
miamidade.gov/parks/
castello-hammock.asp

If you've always wanted the chance to scout for owls at night, you've got one. This is just one of the activities you can sign up for at this 112-acre preserve, which contains a mature tropical hardwood forest that is very popular for birds and butterflies, and those human beings who like to watch them.

## 299 FAIRCHILD TROPICAL BOTANIC GARDEN

10901 Old Cutler Rd
Coral Gables ⑨
+1 305 667 1651
fairchildgarden.org

Not only does this garden – named for the renowned plant explorer David Fairchild – offer guided tram tours of its extensive, impressive 83-acre premises, it also sponsors art exhibits, such as Dale Chihuly installations illuminating the flowers, regularly. Check out the rightly famous Mango and Chocolate festivals in addition to the amazing botanic collections.

## 300 MIAMI BEACH BOTANICAL GARDENS

2000 Convention
Center Drive
South Beach ⑬
+1 305 673 7256
mbgarden.org

This historic site was originally created as the 'Garden Center' in 1962. After suffering from Hurricane Andrew, it was revitalized in 1996 by the Miami Beach Garden Conservancy. Free and open to the public, it now offers everything from orchids to koi ponds, and sponsors arts and cultural programming such as the Japanese Spring Festival.

# 5

# HISTORIC BEACHES

301 **VIRGINIA KEY BEACH PARK**

4020 Virginia
Beach Drive
Virginia Key ⑥
+1 305 960 4600
*virginiakey
beachpark.net*

Established as the 'Colored Only' beach in 1945, this mile-long shoreline contains an antique carousel as well as the oldest plant and animal varieties – many endangered – in the region. View them on the restored hammock trails and wooden boardwalk. Virginia Key also offers a mini train, a modern playground and a Tiki Village for amenities.

302 **BILL BAGGS CAPE FLORIDA STATE PARK**

1200 S Crandon Blvd
Key Biscayne ⑥
+1 305 361 5811
*floridastateparks.org/
park/cape-florida*

The oldest building in Miami-Dade County – a lighthouse constructed in 1825 – stands on these sands, which were also a stop on the Underground Railroad. A regularly recognized 'top ten' beach in the nation, BBCFSP is a rest-and-eat stop for the neotropical birds that migrate through; birders as well as sunbathers and fishermen find this paradise.

### 303 HAULOVER PARK

10800 Collins Ave
Bal Harbour ⑩
+1 305 947 3525
*miamidade.gov/parks/*
*haulover.asp*

Although it was purchased in 1935, Haulover wouldn't be developed completely until 1947 because of WWII. Many myths account for the name, ranging from Prohibition bootleggers to a barefoot mail carrier, all who 'hauled over' items to the mainland before roads were built. Today the beach is famous for flying kites and its nude bathing section.

### 304 SOUTH BEACH

Ocean Drive,
betw 5th and 15th St
South Beach ⑫
*miamiandbeaches.com*

South Beach began as a coconut farm in 1870, and was developed for residences starting in 1910. A decade later, the wealthy poured in for sunshine, bringing with them the art deco architects who left their lasting marks on Ocean Drive, where restoration of these landmark hotels began in the late 1980s and continues today.

### 305 SURFSIDE

Collins Avenue,
betw 87th and 96th St
Town of Surfside ⑩
*townofsurfsidefl.gov*

One mile long, this classic beach town, a loggerhead turtle sanctuary, was frequented by celebrities like Frank Sinatra, Elizabeth Taylor and Winston Churchill. They stayed at the Surf Club, opened in 1930 by tire tycoon Harvey Firestone; today it's a revitalized Four Seasons property where Thomas Keller debuted his first Miami establishment in 2018.

## 5 *terrific*
# GUIDED TOURS

---

### 306 MIAMI BREW BUS

2003 N Miami Ave
Wynwood ③
+1 786 558 3860
*miamibrewbus.com*

Want to tour local breweries? Every Saturday, Miami Brew Bus offers three options, each of which include lots of samples (starting at pick up!), a souvenir glass and more. Tours run from 12 pm to 5.30 pm and cost 60 to 65 dollars per person. Note: Closed-top shoes required; must be 21+.

### 307 TASTE OF MIAMI

AT: MIAMI HELICOPTER
TOURS, MIAMI OPA-LOCKA
EXECUTIVE AIRPORT
14970 NW 42nd Ave
Opa-Locka ①
+1 305 687 0527
*miamihelicopter.com/
helicopter-tours/taste-
of-miami-tour*

Seeing Miami's platinum strips of sand from a helicopter is a whole different proposition than feeling them with your feet. Gain that lofty perspective with this short tour that swoops over Golden, Sunny Isles and Haulover beaches, among others. Priced at 95 dollars per person, it's an elevated adventure well worth the investment.

### 308 FREE HISTORIC TOURS OF COCONUT GROVE
AT: ROYAL PALM TOURS OF MIAMI

2310 SW 11th Terrace
Coral Way ⑦
+1 786 346 3356
coconutgrove.com/
history/tours

Every first and third Saturday of the month, book a free 1,5-hour tour of Miami's oldest municipality. Local history buffs pilot your Cycle Party vehicle, spewing fun facts, music and trivia as you pedal around boho Coco Grove. Groups must be a minimum of six and maximum of 15 people.

### 309 SEGWAY AND BIKE TOURS
AT: BIKE AND ROLL MIAMI

401 Biscayne Blvd
Downtown ④
+1 305 604 0001
bikemiami.com

With one location located at Bayside in the Brickell/Downtown neighborhood and two more in South Beach, this company has a lock on the wheels. If you crave some exercise, sign on for a guided bicycle tour of, say, Wynwood or South Beach. Feeling lazy but want the cooling breezes? Size up a Segway and join a group for an informative ride.

### 310 NEON PADDLE SUNSET TOURS
AT: MIAMI BEACH PADDLEBOARD

1416 18th St
South Beach ⑬
+1 786 428 4402
miamibeachpaddle
board.com/
neon_tour.html

When the sun goes down, the LED lights on the paddle-boards go on, illuminating the water 1,5 meters deep and 4,5 meters around. Paddle past various islands where luxury homes radiate the fiery hues of southern nature, contrasting the city's neon technology. Any way you look at it, it's a very Miami experience.

# 5 top
# TATTOO PARLORS

---

### 311 OCHO PLACAS TATTOO COMPANY

6240 SW 8th St
Flagami ⑮
+1 305 264 0888
*ochoplacastattoo.com*

Founded in 2001 by Jose Carreras, who passed away in 2009, this Calle Ocho shop has been carried on by his former employees, John Vale and Javier Betancourt. Now sought after by celebrities, the skilled inksters at Ocho Placas are in high demand, but the artists themselves remain a humble, hometown crew.

### 312 FAME TATTOOS

1409 W 49th St
Hialeah ⑯
+1 305 303 2025
*fametattoos.com/
realistic-color-tattoos*

These are some wild, realistic and incredibly detailed tattoos, inscribed by fervid *artistes*. The shop and staff reflect an aesthetic of Prohibition chic – slightly naughty but always modish with more than a dash of panache. If you want a tattoo along with a real Magic City experience, Fame is the place to get it.

### 313 IRIS TATTOO STUDIO

2700 N Miami Ave,
#508
Wynwood ③
+1 786 615 9186
iristattoomia.com

Stunning 3D designs, pastel inks and delicate lines define some of the styles at Iris Tattoo. But that's not all that differentiates this place, which feels more like a friend's stylish, comfy apartment than a typical tattoo parlor. Clean, minimalist, striking, and modern, this studio promises – and delivers – a wholistic experience.

### 314 TATTOO & CO.
AT: MIDTOWN TOWER 2

3449 NE 1st Ave
Midtown ③
+1 305 485 0770
tattooandco.com

Because this renowned shop, with its flagship sibling on Bird Road, is located in a hectic urban center, and because the artists are so creative, potential clients absolutely must make an appointment. Walk-ins will be disappointed – especially after seeing the gallery of award-winning work of which these artists are capable. Body piercing also is available.

### 315 INDIAN CREEK TATTOO

6992 Indian Creek Dr
North Beach ⑩
+1 786 315 0222
indiancreektattoo.
squarespace.com

Comfortable and casual, Indian Creek Tattoo caters to both first-time clients who have no idea what they're looking for as much as they do to those who know what they want. Customers can peruse thousands of designs or request a custom piece. The emphasis is on quality and a pleasant experience. Piercing is also available.

---

## 316 SEASPICE

422 NW North
River Drive
Downtown ④
+1 305 440 4200
*seaspicemiami.com*

If you want to catch Beyoncé and Jay Z in the eating act, this renovated warehouse on the Miami River, with dockage that yacht captains jockey over, is the place to do it. Other superstars who quaffed bubbly and feasted on delicacies here include Barbra Streisand, Ryan Phillippe, Marc Anthony and David Beckham.

## 317 PRIME 112

AT: BROWN'S HOTEL
112 Ocean Drive
South Beach ⑫
+1 305 532 8112
*mylesrestaurant
group.com*

This meat palace attracts a ton of the Hollywood elite year round, and for good reason: The beef is Kobe – including the hot dogs and burgers – and the caviar and truffles abound. Top names range from Kim Kardashian and Kanye West to Will Smith to Taraji P. Henson. You'll also spot a lot of athletes.

### 318 ISLAND GARDENS

888 MacArthur Cwy
Watson Island ④
+1 305 531 3747
islandgardens.com

Because this mixed-use restaurant, lounge and retail destination is located on the only private superyacht marina in North America, you can bet that any given night will deliver handfuls of the rich, famous and eclectic out for a night of Ibiza-like partying. These have included Patrick Schwarzenegger, Dennis Rodman, Scottie Pippen and more.

### 319 ART BASEL

Wynwood and
South Beach ③⑫
artbasel.com/
miami-beach

This international visual arts festival transforms both Wynwood and South Beach into a progressive party jam, with luminaries like Madonna, Ariana Grande, Tyson Beckford, Rosario Dawson and Skrillex performing, hosting or appearing at charity events, galleries and museums. While many of the soirees are private, the beaches and restaurants they go to otherwise are public.

### 320 SOUTH BEACH WINE & FOOD FESTIVAL

South Beach ⑫
+1 877 762 3933
sobewff.org

Foodies drool over the possibilities presented by this monster festival, held in giant tents on the sands of South Beach (and in surrounding venues) every February. Celebrity chefs and television personalities ranging from Emeril Lagasse to Guy Fieri to Snoop Dogg host events. Others, like Emilio and Gloria Estefan, simply come for the culinary spirit.

WYNWOOD WALLS

# 80 PLACES TO ENJOY CULTURE

———

# *The 5 most important*
# SMALL GALLERIES

---

### 321 MARKOWICZ FINE ART

110 NE 40th St
Miami Design
District ②
+1 786 615 8158
*markowiczfineart.com*

Never boring and always diverse, this gallery has exhibited a range of art from pop to street by well-known, international artists such as Andy Warhol and Jean Cocteau. Current represented artists/art include Carole A. Feuerman's hyper-realistic sculptures, Markus Klinko's portraits of David Bowie and the whimsical bronzes from Jonathan Delmas.

### 322 DINA MITRANI GALLERY

2620 NW 2nd Ave
Wynwood ③
+1 786 486 7248
*dinamitranigallery.com*

This eponymous gallery features a global roster of renowned photographers, including Pablo Cabado, Shen Chao-Liang, Peggy Nolan and Kanako Sasaki. Mitrani is also a force in the local community, creating opportunities out of her father's former clothing factory.

### 323 MINDY SOLOMON GALLERY

8397 NE 2nd Ave
Little River ②
+1 786 953 6917
*mindysolomon.com*

Located in the Little River Arts District, this lovely space is run by a practising artist, dealer, collector, educator and advocate. As a result, the paintings, photography, sculptures and videos are exhibited in meaningful relationships to each other.

## 324 VALLI ART GALLERY

1924 N Miami Ave
Wynwood ③
+1 305 747 5287
*valliartgallery.com*

Founder Franco Valli's mission is to promote Italian-American art. To that end, he curates pieces by Italian artists, and works closely with them so that he is able to comprehensively communicate with the viewer the meaning of their pieces.

## 325 LOCUST PROJECTS

3852 N Miami Ave
Miami Design
District ②
+1 305 576 8570
*locustprojects.org*

This not-for-profit space encourages wide-ranging, site-specific installations from artists anywhere – regional, national and international – and present them as free, educational opportunities to the public. The organization was founded by Miami artists Elizabeth Withstandley, Westen Charles and COOPER, and was one of the first to spot potential in the Wynwood area.

321 MARKOWICZ FINE ART

# The 5 coolest
# STREET MURALS

---

### 326 WYNWOOD WALLS
**2520 NW 2nd Ave**
**Midtown** ③
**+1 305 531 4411**
*thewynwoodwalls.com*

Street art gets legitimate in this open-air installation museum and gardens for large-scale graffiti. The complex, envisioned by Goldman Properties, includes museum shops and restaurants that all reflect the Miami art scene and Wynwood warehouse vibe. Free of charge, even during Second Saturday Artwalks.

### 327 THE GOOD WALL
**982 SW 8th St**
**Little Havana** ⑦

A play on the word Goodwill, this alleyway gallery was originally painted in 2011 adjacent to the Goodwill resale store that supplies reasonably priced goods for families. The curated art is subject to change, and is related to themes based on Goodwill's mission statement.

### 328 COCONUT GROVE CHILDREN'S MOSAIC – U.S. POST OFFICE MURAL
**3191 Grand Ave**
**Coconut Grove** ⑧

Children drew it; local artists constructed it. The collaboration, led by project architect and mosaicist Cyndy Hill, transformed a bare wall in Coconut Grove into an expression of appreciation for the marine habitat that surrounds the village. It's a loving, colorful tribute that took two years to complete.

### 329 PURVIS YOUNG MURALS
VARIOUS LOCATIONS
*purvisyoung.com*

From Miami's own Liberty City, Purvis Young left a legacy in both museums and on the streets. His murals such as *Everyday Life*, painted in 1984, at the Culmer Overtown Branch Library of the Miami-Dade Public Library and the unnamed installation at the Northside Metrorail Station, painted in 1986, are still intact for viewing.

### 330 HARD ROCK STADIUM
**347 Don Shula Drive**
**Miami Gardens** ①
**+1 305 943 8000**
*hardrockstadium.com*

Jen Stark. Logan Hicks. Dasic Fernández. These are just a few of the street artists commissioned by Miami Dolphins owner to create a unique visual arts impression upon visitors to the renovated home stadium of the city's football team.

326 WYNWOOD WALLS

## *5 of the best places for*
# PERFORMING ARTS

---

### 331 SANDRELL RIVERS THEATER

**6103 NW 7th Ave**
**Little Haiti** ②
**+1 305 284 8800**
*sandrellrivers*
*theater.com*

Named for artist and arts advocate Chief Sandrell Rivers, the theater is devoted to dance and other events that have struggled to find their place in Miami. It's managed by Fantasy Theatre Factory, a company devoted to youth audiences, and The M Ensemble Company, Florida's longest-running African American theater organization, is the resident company.

### 332 ADRIENNE ARSHT CENTER FOR THE PERFORMING ARTS

**1300 Biscayne Blvd**
**Downtown** ④
**+1 305 949 6722**
*arshtcenter.org*

One of the largest performing arts centers in the country, the Arsht is split into two buildings, interrupted by Biscayne Boulevard. It's designed to look like a cruise ship. Interesting architecture aside, it hosts everything from Broadway shows to international symphonies to free family events. Home to the Florida Grand Opera and Miami City Ballet.

### 333 SOUTH MIAMI-DADE CULTURAL ARTS CENTER

**10950 SW 211 St**
**Cutler Bay** ⑭
**+1 786 573 5316**
*smdcac.org*

From ballets by local dance companies to concerts by long-running Latinx acts, this official venue, sponsored by the Miami-Dade County Department of Cultural Affairs, is a great place to catch events that reflect the city's diversity. The South Dade facility, built to fine arts specifics in 2011, also offers education and outreach programs.

### 334 ACTORS' PLAYHOUSE AT THE MIRACLE THEATRE

**280 Miracle Mile**
**Coral Gables** ⑨
**+1 305 444 9293**
*actorsplayhouse.org*

Founded in 1988, this professional theater company performs a full season tailored for the community in a renovated historic venue. It offers live productions for both its 600-seat Mainstage and Children's matinee programs, and each is typically critically acclaimed and award winning. There's also a 300-seat Balcony and a 100-seat Black Box theater.

### 335 MIAMI THEATER CENTER

**9806 NE 2nd Ave**
**Miami Shores** ①
**+1 305 751 9550**
*mtcmiami.org*

Here, resident company Mad Cat Theatre Company and others invited by MTCproductions/MTCpresents entertain the region with a range of performances, from originals to adaptations and poetry to puppetry on the MainStage. Next door, new work is hashed out at the black-box theater in the SandBox Series. Films screened in partnership with O Cinema.

# 5 exciting
# INDEPENDENT CINEMAS

---

### 336 O CINEMA
**500 71st St**
**North Beach** ⑩
**+1 786 207 1919**

If you're craving an independent film, art flick, an international film, or a classic, then O is it. With a second location on South Beach and special pairings throughout the year with other cultural programs, there's always something to see.

### 337 SILVERSPOT CINEMA
**300 SE 3rd St, #100**
**Downtown** ④
**+1 305 536 5000**
*downtownmiami.*
*silverspot.net*

Here's a tip: You can now see an independent or foreign film (or okay, even a Hollywood blockbuster) while leaning back in a recliner with a glass of wine and plate of pan-seared salmon. Welcome to Silverspot, where service comes with the big screen, and even extends to operas, ballets and concerts.

### 338 CORAL GABLES ART CINEMA
**260 Aragon Avenue**
**Coral Gables** ⑨
**+1 786 385 9689**
*gablescinema.com*

This large, modern theater is a collaboration between the City of Coral Gables (which owns the building) and the nonprofit Coral Gables Cinematique. One of the more comfy spots to see first-run, independent features and documentaries, international films and classics. It also shows the Annual Miami International Children's Film Festival.

### 339 MDC'S TOWER THEATER

1508 SW 8th St
Little Havana ⑦
+1 305 237 2463
*towertheatermiami.com*

The Tower debuted as an English-language cinema in 1926, but switched to Spanish when Cuban *exilios* arrived. It got a new lease on cultural life in 2002 when Miami Dade College revitalized it. Now it screens both Spanish-language and English-language films, subtitled in Spanish. It also sponsors lectures, performances and exhibits.

### 340 THE BILL COSFORD CINEMA

AT: UNIVERSITY OF MIAMI
SCHOOL OF COMMUNICATION
5030 Brunson Drive
Memorial Building 227
Coral Gables ⑨
+1 305 284 4627
(box office)
+1 305 284 9838
(showtimes)
*cosfordcinema.com*

Serving both the university and the greater population for more than 60 years, this cinema shows a variety of formats, from 35 mm to high-definition digital. Both an educational experience and an art facility, it brings in actors and directors like Jon Landis and Kevin Spacey for interactive lectures, and runs the Canes Film Festival.

339 MDC'S TOWER THEATER

# 5 things to do at
# PÉREZ ART MUSEUM MIAMI

---

**1103 Biscayne Boulevard**
**Downtown** ④
**+1 305 375 3000**
*pamm.org*

### 341 TOUR: FREE AND GUIDED
*pamm.org/learn/tours*

Tours include exploring the Herzog & de Meuron architecture, Brazilian green heartwood deck with hanging gardens and galleries of Latin American and Caribbean art. At 45 minutes in English or Spanish, they're available daily at 11 am, noon and 2.30 pm, and 6.30 on Thursday evenings. Special needs can be accommodated.

### 342 MAKE ART: PAMM STUDIO PROGRAMS
*pamm.org/studio*

Take workshops – tailored with activities for all ages. Or go lone wolf and sketch (pencil only) in the galleries, then outside to investigate the 67 sustainable, hanging gardens on the veranda, created by Patrick Blanc. The deck is festooned with 54.700 plants, comprising 77 plant species, that can withstand category 5 hurricane-force winds.

### 343 EAT: VERDE

+1 786 345 5697
*pamm.org/dining*

Enjoy brunch or lunch at this indoor-outdoor restaurant run by the catering arm of Stephen Starr's group. Dishes range from a rock shrimp pizza with broccoli rabe to crispy *mahi-mahi* tacos. Admission to the museum is not required for supping and sipping. Dinner on Thursdays only.

### 344 LISTEN AND LEARN: THURSDAY EVENINGS

*pamm.org/calendar*

On Thursdays, PAMM extends its hours until 9 pm. Verde remains open for dinner, and live music or DJs on the deck also add to the experience. In addition, check the calendar for extant performances, lectures and film screenings in the on-site theater.

### 345 SHOP: SOUVENIRS

*shop.pamm.org*

Not gonna lie – this is a great museum shop, as colorful and eclectic as PAMM and Miami itself. Take home items from the 'Miami Kitsch Collection' or PAMM signature products like the 'Didactic T-Shirt'. You can even find the ultra-hometown Wynwood Coloring Book here.

# 5 inspiring
# SPECIALTY MUSEUMS

---

### 346 BURGER MUSEUM BY BURGER BEAST

**450 NW 37th Ave
West Flagler ⑦
+1 305 305 3999
burgerbeast.com/
burger-museum**

A museum devoted to hamburgers? Well, it makes sense if you're founder Sef Gonzalez, who calls himself 'Burger Beast', and is not only an expert on every slider and sandwich in the city, but has a collection of memorabilia to prove it. Pop into its warm, toasty bun at Magic City Casino.

### 347 BLACK POLICE PRECINCT COURTHOUSE & MUSEUM

**480 NW 11th St
Overtown ⑦
+1 305 329 2513
historicalblack
precinct.org**

Too often overlooked, African-American history is preserved here with a special mission in mind: to record the challenges and accomplishments of the Black police officers who were on duty pre-Civil Rights era. Displays feature the bicycles they used, Black Precinct jail cells, original plaques, historic photos and more from the 1940s, 1950s and 1960s.

## 348 JEWISH MUSEUM OF FLORIDA – FIU

**301 Washington Ave**
**South Beach** ⑫
**+1 305 672 5044**
*jmof.fiu.edu*

Before any group that currently defines the immigrant experience appeared and settled in Miami, there were the Jews. This museum is dedicated to their culture and history of worldwide discrimination. Exhibits range from amusing (food, fashion) to truly chilling (genocide).

## 349 WINGS OVER MIAMI AIR MUSEUM

AT: MIAMI EXECUTIVE
AIRPORT
**14710 SW 128th St**
**Kendall** ⑭
**+1 305 233 5197**
*wingsovermiami.com*

Plane buffs love this place, which is located in a hangar on a runway. An homage to the history of flight, the 'exhibits' include vintage aircraft from the military, civilian and commercial realms, and almost all of them can fly. Most flight activity takes place on weekends.

## 350 WORLD EROTIC ART MUSEUM

**1205 Washington Ave**
**South Beach** ⑫
**+1 305 532 9336**
*weam.com*

It makes sense that sexy South Beach would be the home to the only museum in the U.S. dedicated to fine erotic art. It was founded on the personal collection of Naomi Wilzig. Today the museum showcases more than 4000 pieces, dating from 300 BCE to the present.

# 5 awesome
# ARTS FAIRS

351 **CHAMBERSOUTH SOUTH MIAMI ART FESTIVAL**
**Sunset Dr, between U.S. Hwy 1 and SW 57th Ave**
**South Miami ⑭**
**+1 305 661 1621**
*chambersouth.com/ miami-art-festival*

This juried show features more than 100 artists from all over the world working in such diverse mediums as ceramics, digital art, textiles, glass, metalwork and photography. If you can conceive it, you can bet it will be there. Free and open to the public, the event includes culinary and musical entertainment.

352 **ART MIAMI**
AT: ONE HERALD PLAZA
**At NE 14th St on Biscayne Bay betw the Venetian and McArthur Cwys**
**Downtown ④**
*artmiamifair.com*

More than 75.000 lovers of 20th- and 21st-century art visit this fair, which was established in the late 1980s. It showcases galleries and artists and attracts dealers and curators from all over the world during what is now commonly known as Art Week, December 5 to 10, during Art Basel.

### 353 CONTEXT ART MIAMI

AT: ONE HERALD PLAZA
**At NE 14th St on
Biscayne Bay betw
the Venetian &
McArthur Cwys
Downtown** ④
**+1 305 517 7977**
*contextartmiami.com*

This sibling to Art Miami debuted in 2012 in order to present emerging and mid-career talent, as well as those artists outside the mainstream. It takes place from December 5-10, and attracts more than 80.000 people. Park in the garage across the street and hop on shuttles to go between various Art Week fairs.

### 354 AQUA ART MIAMI

AT: AQUA HOTEL
**1530 Collins Avenue
South Beach** ⑫
**+1 305 517 7977**
*aquaartmiami.com*

Scheduled during Art Week from December 6 to 10, this art fair – related to Art Miami – is set in the boutique Aqua Hotel. The intimate format of rooms-turned-galleries, and crowds spilling into the lush courtyard, makes the contemporary art, brought by more than 45 representatives, even more inviting.

### 355 RED DOT MIAMI

**1700 NE 2nd Ave
(at NE 17th St)
Edgewater** ③
**+1 831 747 0112**
*reddotmiami.com*

While this fair also takes place during Art Week, December 6 to 10, it sets itself apart by being themed – a different theme each year – and offering more interactive opportunities for its audience. The art includes all genres and mediums, and features performance pieces, installations, Art Labs, Art Talks and more.

# The 5 most amazing
# MUSIC FESTIVALS

—————

### 356 MIAMI MUSIC WEEK
VARIOUS LOCATIONS
*miamimusicweek.com*

Although it's not exactly a secret, the week-long celebration of EDM called Miami Music Week (MMW) is ever-evolving, and you never know what's going to happen. For instance, in 2020, homegrown festival Ultra Music Festival merges with MMW for the first time as the grand finale. Overall, more than 1200 artists and 200.000 fans attend.

### 357 III POINTS
AT: MANA WYNWOOD
**318 NW 23rd St**
**Wynwood** ③
*iiipoints.com*

This multi-day, Miami-born festival combines musical performances from eclectic international groups such as Gorillaz, Lykke Li, Thievery Corporation and M83 with new, experiential technology exhibits and grand-scale visual art installations. Being on the showgrounds every October is so multisensory and multidimensional, it's like living in a virtual reality game.

### 358 ROLLING LOUD

AT: HARD ROCK STADIUM
**347 Don Shula Dr
Miami Gardens** ①
*rollingloud.com*

Hip-hop and rap artists from emerging to made-it status take multiple stages for three days straight at this born-and-raised Miami festival. Each May it becomes more popular, attracting bigger and better acts, including Young Thug, Migos, A$AP Rocky, Future and Kendrick Lamar. All ages, rain or shine.

### 359 THE CORAL GABLES HISPANIC CULTURAL FESTIVAL

AT: CORAL GABLES
CITY HALL
**405 Biltmore Way
Coral Gables** ⑨
**+1 305 667 0577**
*gableshispanic
festival.com*

Celebrate all things Hispanic, including the many different styles of music, from Uruguyan folk to Spanish flamenco to Latin pop, at this annual two-day October event. The schedule, though subject to change, is posted beforehand, so you can make sure to catch a favorite act – or see one you've never heard before. Free admission.

### 360 MIAMI MUSIC FESTIVAL

VARIOUS LOCATIONS
*miamimusicfestival.com*

With performances all over Miami, the MMF, which launched in 2013, is a summer celebration of young classical musicians. From early June until late July, international applicants from conservatories and universities perform in in full operas, symphonic concerts, piano concerts, recitals, chamber orchestra and musical theater performances.

## The 5 best
# STREET FAIRS

---

### 361 CALLE OCHO FESTIVAL

SW 8th St
(12th to 27th Ave)
Little Havana ⑦
+1 305 644 8888
*carnavalmiami.com/
event-view/calle-ocho*

For more than 40 years, the Kiwanis Club of Little Havana produces this March event that celebrates Hispanic culture. Live music, colorful costumes and competitions – who has the best Cuban sandwich or *croqueta*? – attract record-breaking crowds that dance down the street annually. Expect distinctly tropical drinks, too!

### 362 CARNAVAL ON THE MILE

Miracle Mile
Coral Gables ⑨
*carnavalmiami.com/
event-view/carnaval-
on-the-mile-2017*

It might seem like a warm-up for the grand Calle Ocho, as it takes place a week or two before, and is also sponsored by Kiwanis. But this Coral Gables festival has its own traditions. The street party takes place on Miracle Mile and focuses music and art as well as good eats and drinks.

### 363 KING MANGO STRUT

Coconut Grove
*kingmangostrut.org*

Uniquely Miami, this avant-garde parade started in 1981 as a sarcastic response to the Orange Bowl tradition. Now, with its satire well established, the party outdoes itself with self-deprecating, jesting protests. Anything funny goes, and anyone can apply to participate. After the parade, the music begins to welcome the new year.

### 364 ART DECO WEEKEND

Ocean Drive (betw 5th and 13th St)
South Beach ⑫
+1 305 672 2014
*artdecoweekend.com*

For more than 40 years, South Beach has been celebrating the art, architecture and era that define its Historic District. Activities include tours of Ocean Drive and Collins Avenue, classic car shows, exhibits and lectures, and of course plenty of vendors offering items for sale. There's even a 'Bark Deco Dog Show'!

### 365 VIERNES CULTURALES

Domino Plaza (Calle Ocho, between 13th and 17th Avenues)
Little Havana ⑦
+1 305 643 5500
*viernesculturales.org*

This amazing celebration of Cuban arts and culture takes place every third Friday of the month in the fresh air of Little Havana. Enjoy domino games, cigar rolling, live music, dancing, food, arts and crafts, and more. It's a scene that you think can't be repeated – but is, every month.

# 5 small venues for
# LIVE MUSIC

---

### 366 CHURCHILL'S PUB
**5501 NE 2nd Ave**
**Little Haiti** ②
**+1 305 757 1807**
*churchillspub.com*

An 18+ venue, this Miami institution has been showcasing live bands of all genres, sizes and popularity – many have gone on to (or come down from) stardom – since 1979. Chill to jazz, folk, rock, alternative and funk.

### 367 NORTH BEACH BANDSHELL
**7275 Collins Ave**
**North Beach** ⑩
**+1 786 453 2897**
*northbeach bandshell.com*

This MiMo jewel of an amphitheater, built in 1961, is part of the North Shore Historic District. Renovated in 2011, it's run by the Rhythm Foundation, which books acts ranging from indie Latin American singer-songwriters to samba. Before a show, have a seat at Bandshell Park's dominoes pavilion or stroll the Beach Walk.

### 368 SWEAT RECORDS
**5505 NE 2nd Ave**
**Little Haiti** ②
**+1 786 693 9309**
*sweatrecordsmiami.com*

A mixed bag of music paraphernalia, cool duds, coffee bar with vegan baked goods and event space, Sweat was the first independent vinyl record store to open in Miami. Watch the web page for who's playing live – it's usually a local band – or vinyl release listening parties.

369 **MARTHA / MARY CONCERTS**
AT: LA MERCED CHAPEL & CORPUS CHRISTI CHURCH
**3220 NW 7 Ave**
**Allapattah** ③
**+1 305 458 0111**
*marthamary*
*concerts.org*

For decades, St. Martha's Church has presented reliably awesome global programming in the fields of classical and jazz music at 'movie ticket prices' (with free popcorn). Now located in a Spanish baroque chapel and larger adjacent church, it continues outreach to schools and community; no one is turned anyone away for inability to pay.

370 **LAGNIAPPE**
**3425 NE 2nd Ave**
**Midtown** ③
**+1 305 576 0108**
*lagniappehouse.com*

Live music every night, with a broad range of appeal – swing, bluegrass, folk, country, jazz, funk, soul – and during weekend afternoons in the Garden. Enjoy the residencies like the Wynwood String Band who play every Thursday night, and other local regulars.

366 **CHURCHILL'S PUB**

# 5

# NIGHTCLUBS AND LOUNGES

---

### 371 MYNT

**1921 Collins Ave**
**South Beach** ⑬
**+1 305 532 0727**
*myntlounge.com*

It's no secret that this long-running nightclub, luxe to the max, has one of the strictest door policies in town. If you want to dance to house music under those LED strobes with the other nightlife hoi polloi, it's dress – or in the case of South Beach, un-dress – to impress.

### 372 MR. KREAM ICE CREAM LOUNGE

**2400 N Miami Ave**
**Wynwood** ③
**+1 786 659 4541**
*mrkreamwynwood.com*

Kids Rule Everything Around Me. Co-owner Ari Kalimi, who is also DJ Affect, makes good on that acronym/motto by theming every ice-cream product in the shop to the hip-hop generation he serves. Enjoy flavors like 'A$AP Rocky Road' or 'Snoopstachio'; this place is a hoot and delish to boot.

### 373 MR. JONES

**320 Lincoln Road**
**South Beach** ⑬
**+1 305 602 3117**
*mrjonesmiami.com*

One of the most decadent nightclubs on South Beach, Mr. Jones has kicked it up so high the partying is stratospheric. For aficionados who know their DJs, Purge Tuesdays and Varsity Fridays are all about hip-hop. But it's the themed, music-driven bottle service parades that grab the attention of drinkers and listeners alike.

## 374 **VILLA AZUR**

**309 23rd St**
**South Beach** ⑫
**+1 305 763 8688**
*villaazurmiami.com*

This elegant Mediterranean restaurant and lounge is run by a partnership of nightlife veterans. Thus the entertainment programming is ever changing, from DJ sets to operatic performances to sax solos. Open since 2012, it's dependable for fine dining on artichoke gnocchi and seat dancing the night away.

## 375 **BRICK**

**187 NW 28th St**
**Wynwood** ③
**+1 786 467 1205**
*brickmia.com*

DJ Camilo. DJ Retrokidd. DJ Selecta Renegade. And so it goes. Graffiti art on the outside of the building; beats and craft beers of all nationalities inside, plus cocktails that change with the seasons – such as they are in the subtropics. Open until 3 am Wednesday to Sunday.

# The 5 best
# LITERARY VENUES

---

### 376 BOOKS & BOOKS
**265 Aragon Ave**
**Coral Gables** ⑨
**+1 305 442 4408**
*booksandbooks.com*

Consistently named one of the best independent bookstores in the country, Mitchell Kaplan's Books & Books sets the stage for every writer in town or who comes through on tour. It hosts more than 60 events per month, from best-selling politicians to YA authors.

### 377 MIAMI-DADE PUBLIC LIBRARY SYSTEM
**Main Library**
**101 W Flagler St**
**Downtown** ④
**+1 305 375 2878**
*mdpls.org/branches/*
*main-library.html*

Whether you're looking to take a work-shop or simply listen to an author read, the city's libraries are some of the best – and least utilized – places to do it. The main branch offers plenty of opportunities, including exhibits and anthologies of work, as do the community locations, from both resident and visiting authors.

### 378 NATIONAL YOUNGARTS FOUNDATION
**2100 Biscayne Blvd**
**Edgewater** ③
**+1 305 377 1140**
*youngarts.org*

This fantastic organization assists teenagers in all the arts achieve recognition and mastery. Part of their mission is bringing in award-winning talent to model, events to which the community is invited to buy tickets. See the likes of Robert Redford and Natalie Diaz, and then listen to the emerging young voices.

### 379 FIU BISCAYNE BAY CAMPUS BOOKSTORE

AT: WOLFE UNIVERSITY CENTER, 1ST FLOOR
**3000 NE 145th St
North Miami** ①
**+1 305 919 5580**
*english.fiu.edu/
creative-writing/events*

Florida International University's north campus bookstore is a low-key place to spot the city's literati, many of whom teach here, and visiting writers. The renowned Creative Writing Program holds its Writers on the Bay Reading Series here, which has presented Ann Hood, Thrity Umrigar and Rigoberto Gonzalez.

### 380 MIAMI BOOK FAIR

AT: MIAMI-DADE COLLEGE, WOLFSON CAMPUS
**600 Biscayne Blvd
Downtown** ④
**+1 305 237 3258**
*miamibookfair.com*

This eight-day event takes place every third weekend of November. Founded by Miami Dade College and partners like Books & Books in 1984, it is the most noteworthy literary festivals in the country, and attracts authors from all over the world to read from their most recent publications.

376 BOOKS & BOOKS

# SEASONAL CARNIVALS

—————

### 381 SANTA'S ENCHANTED FOREST

**7900 SW 40th St**
**Olympia Heights** ⑮
**+1 305 559 9689**
*santasenchanted*
*forest.com*

This carnival may be themed around the idea of Christmas, but it's a long holiday. Beginning in November, you can take advantage of more than 100 rides, games and shows. The trees, lights and decorations, which have only been getting more elaborate since the early 1980s, are attractions in themselves.

### 382 MIAMI-DADE COUNTY FAIR AND EXPOSITION

AT: FAIR EXPO CENTER
**10901 SW 24th St**
**University Park** ⑮
**+1 305 223 7060**
*thefair.me*

A beloved Miami tradition. Take a country fair with its agricultural, fitness, arts and other competitions, and mix it with a high-tech whirl of thriller rollercoasters and other rides. That's what's known as 'The Fair'. While sponsored events take place all year, the Fair Expo runs for a few weeks every March to April.

## 383 ST. ROSE OF LIMA CARNIVAL

**415 NE 105th St**
**Miami Shores** ①
**+1 305 751 0539**
*stroseoflima*
*miamishores.org*

Every January, this community carnival attracts visitors from all over the city. A widely anticipated weekend, it is a fundraiser for the school, which devotes its entire grounds to rides, games, musical acts, food stands, raffles and more. Especially fun for families and teens on their own.

## 384 HOUSE OF HORROR HAUNTED CARNIVAL

LOCATION ANNOUNCED
ON WEBSITE
*houseofhorrorpark.com*

As if it's not enough to be scared to death by plunging carnival rides and circus sideshows, this spread-out haunted house, with 25 or so ghostly scenes played out by spooky characters, runs from late September through early November. Still breathing? Tickets for the Phantasma Music Festival, a '2 Day Killer' experience, are separate.

## 385 EASTER FUN DAY

AT: CAULEY SQUARE
HISTORIC VILLAGE
**22400 Old Dixie Hwy**
**Redland** ⑬⑭
**+1 305 258 3543**
*cauleysquare.com/*
*events*

A lovely introduction to this charming, antique village, this carnival is on the mild side, not the wild side, for young children who want to ride a pony, take a train ride and jump in bounce houses. Eggs filled with candy are hidden in the ornamental gardens. Ten dollars per child.

## 5 *places to experience*
# LATIN CULTURE

---

**386 KOUBEK CENTER**
AT: MIAMI DADE COLLEGE
**2705 SW 3rd St**
**Little Havana** ⑦
**+1 305 237 7750**
*koubekcenter.org*

This historic mansion and its gardens were acquired by the city's public college with a specific mission in mind – to promote the Spanish-American diaspora through the arts. The structure was turned into stages, galleries, literary arts opportunities and lecture halls. Now, from films to children's theater classes, there's plenty Spanish-American learning going on.

**387 CUBAOCHO MUSEUM & PERFORMING ARTS CENTER**
**1465 SW 8th St, #106**
**Little Havana** ⑦
**+1 305 285 5880**
*cubaocho.com*

More like a gallery than a museum, as the exhibits continually change, this enterprising business model takes advantage of all its space to also display a large collection of Cuban memorabilia. In addition to live music performances, the venue hosts lectures and book launches, and sells fine art prints in its shop.

## 388 CISNEROS FONTANALS ART FOUNDATION

**1018 N Miami Ave**
**Downtown** ④
**+1 305 415 6343**
*cifo.org*

Called CIFO, this ambitious institution launches for the season every September with a new exhibit under the auspices of its Grants and Commissions Program Collection. The contemporary Latin American artists, either emerging or mid-career, are selected to expose them to curators, collectors and others with influence who visit the Miami art world.

## 389 AMERICAN MUSEUM OF THE CUBAN DIASPORA

**1200 Coral Way**
**Coral Way** ⑥
**+1 305 529 5400**
*thecuban.org*

This museum tells the story of the Cuban revolution through art. The exhibits reveal just how heartbreaking it is to leave family, friends and home-land behind forever, and they also show the challenges and the joys of discovering new lives in far-flung places – all through the medium of visual arts. Exile explained; brilliance realized.

## 390 MAXIMO GOMEZ PARK

**801 SW 15th Ave**
**Little Havana** ⑦
**+1 305 859 2717**
*miamigov.com/parks*

Casually nicknamed 'Domino Park' because of the number of older Cuban men who play the game there, this neighborhood spot has become quite a colorful attraction. Benches were added a couple of years ago for those who want to watch the action, which can get intense; domino-themed tiles were also installed. 9 am to 6 pm daily.

# 5 sites for understanding
# HAITIAN HERITAGE

---

**391 HAITIAN HERITAGE MUSEUM**

4141 NE 2nd Ave, #105-C
Little Haiti ②
+1 305 371 5988
*haitianheritage museum.org*

This flourishing institution was born in 2004 as an educational platform to connect Haitian Americans with their artistic, historic and cultural roots. The exhibits, films, readings, lectures and musical performances allow every visitor to dig deeply into Haiti's impactful heritage.

**392 LITTLE HAITI CULTURAL COMPLEX**

212-260 NE 59th Terrace
Little Haiti ②
+1 305 960 2969
*littlehaiticultural center.com*

There are so many wonderful components to this performing arts center, exhibition space, outreach and education space, and community hall. Programming ranges from one-offs like a pop-up Wyclef Jean concert to regular events like the Sounds of Little Haiti festivals every third Friday night of the month, and the Caribbean Market Day every second Saturday.

**393 LIBRERI MAPOU**

5919 NE 2nd Ave
Little Haiti ②
+1 305 757 9922
*mapoubooks.com*

This bookstore stocks work in several languages, including Creole and French, and promotes it by partnering with Miami Dade College to present The Little Haiti Book Festival. It also highlights Haitian arts and crafts.

### 394 HAITIAN COMPAS FESTIVAL

**2217 NW 5th Ave**
**Wynwood** ③
**+1 305 573 0371**
*haitiancompas*
*festival.com*

Branded just before the turn of the Millennium, this festival – one of the biggest Haitian music events in the nation – gets better every year. Look for top konpa acts like Djakout, Ada, Steph Lecor and Kreyol La to perform over a two-day period every May at Mana Wynwood.

### 395 TOUSSAINT LOUVERTURE MEMORIAL STATUE

**6136 N Miami Ave**
**Little Haiti** ②

Commissioned by the City of Miami, the seven-foot-tall statue of General Toussaint Louverture stands in a small park at the corner of N Miami Avenue and 62nd Street. The Haitian icon, who led the revolution against the French colonists to free the country, is often the site of peaceful demonstrations and vigils.

395 TAP TAP RESTAURANT

# 5 sites for admiring Miami's
# NATIVE AMERICAN
## *background*

---

### 396 MICCOSUKEE RESORT & CASINO

**500 SW 177th Ave
Krome Avenue
Reservation** ⑬⑭
**+1 305 222 4600**
*miccosukee.com*

Sure, you can stack your Bingo cards, try your hand at high-stakes poker, and pull the arm on plenty of gaming machines. But what's really interesting here are all the displays of Miccosukee culture that exist in between the entertainments. The authentic exhibits are just a glimpse of what's been preserved, and what's been lost.

### 397 MICCOSUKEE INDIAN VILLAGE

**Everglades NP, US-41
Tamiami Trail
Reservation** ⑬
**+1 305 552 8365**
*miccosukee.com/
indian-village*

Even if you don't want to be the volunteer chosen to hold closed the snout of a large alligator, you can have an adventure at the Village. Learn about basket weaving and beadwork. Tour the museum. And sample fry bread and frogs' legs, which do taste like chicken.

### 398 THE MIAMI CIRCLE

AT: BRICKELL POINT SITE
**401 Brickell Ave
Brickell** ⑤
*miamicircle.org*

This Tequesta archaeological artifact was discovered during preparation for building a skyscraper in downtown Miami in 1998. It dates back to 2000 years before the arrival of the Spanish. No one's entirely sure of the purpose, but it's been preserved so that everybody can take a gander and a guess.

### 399 HISTORYMIAMI MUSEUM

**101 W Flagler St**
**Downtown** ④
**+1 305 375 1492**
*historymiami.org*

Find fascinating tribal artifacts in the 37.000-item Object Collection of this reliable museum. In the Seminole Collection in particular, dolls, beads, baskets, patchwork and even wooden dugout canoes are on exhibit. It's a glimpse into the Florida way of life before the Europeans and air-conditioning invaded.

### 400 PAHAYOKEE OVERLOOK

AT: EVERGLADES
NATIONAL PARK
**40001 State Rd 9336**
**Homestead** ⑬
**+1 305 242 7700**
*www.nps.gov/ever*

The Miccosukee and Seminole tribes called the Everglades home long before they were forced onto government-designated reservations. Visit Pahayokee (Seminole for 'grassy river'), a boardwalk and lookout tower, to gain some perspective and photograph some of the best views in Everglades National Park.

398 THE MIAMI CIRCLE

miami **children's** museum
THE POTAMKIN FAMILY BUILDING

# 20 THINGS TO DO
# WITH CHILDREN

---

# The 5 best places with
# WILDLIFE

---

**401 ZOO MIAMI**

1 Zoo Boulevard
12400 SW 152nd St
Deerwood ⑭
+1 305 251 0400
*zoomiami.org*

Feed giraffes, parrots or an Indian rhino. Journey down the Asian River Life exhibit. Catch the lion pride at rest; the lowland gorillas in action. Whatever you do, plan your day – this is 750 acres of cage-less space for more than 500 animal species.

**402 JUNGLE ISLAND**

1111 Parrot Jungle
Trail
Watson Island ④
+1 305 400 7000
*jungleisland.com*

View more than 300 tropical birds, including a trained cassowary, and rare animals, such as the interspecies ligers and tions, on more than two kilometers of trails or at the wildlife shows. Bring a bathing suit (in season) for splashing around the Rainforest Riptide, an incredible water playground on Parrot Cove Beach.

**403 MONKEY JUNGLE**

14805 SW 216th St
Redland ⑬⑭
+1 305 235 1611
*monkeyjungle.com*

This 30-acre preserve was started in 1935 with just six Java macaques. Now more than 300 primates, many endangered, live expansively in what is essentially a curated rainforest while the humans walk through on protected boardwalks. Watch the Java troupe, now numbering in the 90s, dive for food in their pond.

### 404 THE ORIGINAL COOPERTOWN AIRBOAT

22700 SW 8th St
Miami ⑬
+1 305 226 6048
*coopertownairboats.com*

Guided airboats, steered by knowledge-able guides, skim over sawgrass in mere inches of water in search of native flora and fauna. You can spot everything from great blue herons to alligators. Afterward, dine on frog legs, alligator and catfish in the on-site restaurant for an additional authentic experience.

### 405 ZOOLOGICAL WILDLIFE FOUNDATION

16225 SW 172nd Ave
Richmond West ⑭
+1 305 969 3696
*zoologicalwildlife foundation.com*

This amazing five-acre rescue and rehabilitation sanctuary offers tours of the premises to support its education efforts. See big cats, lemurs, sloths, giant anteaters – everything from camels to cockatoos – who are endangered or have been removed from unhealthy situations. You can also book play sessions with juvenile felines and primates. Reservations are mandatory.

404 THE ORIGINAL COOPERTOWN AIRBOAT

# *The 5 best family*
# BEACHES, WATER-PARKS AND POOLS

---

## 406 VENETIAN POOL

2701 De Soto Blvd
Coral Gables ⑨
+1 305 460 5306
coralgables.com

Chiseled from a limestone quarry pit and complete with grottos and waterfalls this freshwater pool is every child's pirate/princess fantasy playground. There are gorgeous backdrops for sunbathing, selfie-taking teens, and historic architecture highlights for adults. On the National Register of Historic Places. Kids must be 3+.

## 407 CRANDON PARK VISITOR AND NATURE CENTER

6747 Crandon Blvd
Key Biscayne ⑥
+1 305 361 6767
miamidade.gov/parks

The long, wide, lagoon-style beaches – two miles of them – have long-range visibility and lead to calm waters, protected by an offshore sandbar. Sloping sands allow for little ones to wade. Lifeguard stands, water sports and food concessions, picnic areas with tables and grills, and plentiful parking make an all-day outing safe and easy.

## 408 GRAPELAND WATER PARK

1550 NW 37th Ave
Flagami ⑦
+1 305 960 2950
*archive.miamigov.com/
grapeland*

Four attractions provide something for everyone. Shipwreck Island is for little ones while Pirate's Plunge is for older kids, but both provide slides, water cannons and splash fountains. Captain's Lagoon is a large, heated pool; the Buccaneer River Ride offers a relaxing float on an inflatable tube. Free life vests available; swim diapers for purchase.

## 409 MCDONALD WATER PARK

7505 W 12th Avenue
Hialeah ⑯
+1 305 818 9164
*hialeahfl.gov*

In addition to the mandatory activity pool, this park features a 305-meter lazy river that takes its riders, ensconced on inner tubes, through a tunnel under a waterfall. A wave pool is also the only of its kind in Miami-Dade County. Catch your breath or consume snacks from the concession at umbrella-shaded tables.

## 410 BUCKY DENT WATER PARK

2240 West 60th St
Hialeah ⑯
+1 305 818 2990
*hialeahfl.gov*

The specialties here include twin water slides, so you can race someone to the bottom, and an Olympic-size pool with zero-depth entry, so toddlers can splash in one end and serious swimmers can train elsewhere. And the interactive water playground is safe aquatic fun for everyone.

## 5 fun

# PARKS, PLAYGROUNDS AND MUSEUMS

### 411 MIAMI CHILDREN'S MUSEUM

980 MacArthur Cwy
Watson Island ④
+1 305 373 5437
miamichildrens
museum.org

This creatively crafted facility is pure entertainment. Exhibits weave the natural environment, the arts and the multicultural community together. Explore a cruise ship. Bring drawings to life in a virtual aquarium. Shop at a play supermarket or operate a crane at the Port of Miami.

### 412 IGI PLAYGROUND

12885 Biscayne
Boulevard, #3
North Miami ①
+1 786 434 5706
igiplayground
miami.com

Built like a giant pirate ship, this indoor playground features slides, crawl tubes, trampolines, a ball pit, and so much to climb even a real sailor might have trouble. Additional apparatus and play tables provide safe spaces for toddlers.

## 413 SOUNDSCAPE PARK/ WALLCAST®

AT: NEW WORLD CENTER

500 17th St
South Beach ⑬
+1 305 673 3330
+1 800 517 3331
*nws.edu*

The domain of New World Center, home to New World Symphony, a world-class training orchestra, this green space is perfect for a picnic while you watch a concert or family-friendly movie outside on the high-tech WALLCAST®. Spread a blanket and bring some comfy sweaters. No one minds if little ones fall asleep.

## 414 PHILLIP AND PATRICIA FROST MUSEUM OF SCIENCE

AT: MUSEUM PARK

1101 Biscayne Blvd
Downtown ④
+1 305 434 9600
*frostscience.org*

Whether you're into the realm of outer space or the world under the sea, this is the place to observe exhibits, shows and programs. The Frost Planetarium is as high tech as NASA. The interactive, three-level Aquarium is simply one of a kind, re-creating the Gulf Stream, the Everglades and more.

## 415 GOLD COAST RAILROAD MUSEUM

12450 SW 152nd St
Deerwood ⑭
+1 305 253 0063
*goldcoastrailroad
museum.org*

Train buffs get a big kick out of this collection of 40+ real-world antique railcars, cabooses and locomotives. A couple of these are operational, so the museum offers rides most weekends, depending on crew and equipment availability. Other exhibits include model trains and Thomas the Tank play tables. Located next to Zoo Miami.

# 5

# BIG ADVENTURES

---

### 416 ADRENALINE JUNKY RIDE

AT: JET BOAT MIAMI/
SEA ISLE MARINA

1635 N Bayshore Dr
Edgewater ③
+1 954 397 6079
jetboatmiami.com

Few things are more exciting than speeding across the bay in a cigarette-style boat – except for when the captain throws in those 360-degree spins. This 30-minute ride also allows you to see the exclusive homes on Star and Fisher islands. Not for the weak of heart or stomach. Departs from Sea Isle Marina.

### 417 X-TREME ROCK CLIMBING CENTER

13972 SW 139th Ct
West Kendall ⑭
+1 305 233 6623
x-tremerock.com

Learn how or build your skills at this rock-climbing gym. Routes are frequently changed by experts so that there's always something new to test your strength. Competitions, kids' and adult classes, fitness and yoga centers, and a gear shop are available.

### 418 CORAL CASTLE MUSEUM

28655 S Dixie Hwy
Homestead ⑬
+1 305 248 6345
coralcastle.com

An engineering and architectural mystery, this structure and its 'furnishings' were carved entirely out of coral over the course of 28 years. No one can figure out how Ed Leedskalnin constructed items such as a 9-ton coral rock gate by himself – with homemade tools to boot. A fascinating stop on the way to the Keys.

### 419 NINJA LOUNGE

14401 NE 20th Lane
North Miami ①
+1 786 590 5000
ninjalounge.com

Trampoline courts. Ropes. Obstacle courses. Parkour and aerial silks workshops. Handstand and cartwheel clinics. Whether you're playing dodgeball and basketball or learning a new fitness skill, try it while bouncing off the walls – literally.

### 420 SUNRISE BALLOONS MIAMI

1881 Washington Ave
South Beach ⑫
+1 305 747 1951
balloonmiami.com
DEPARTURES AT:
THE EUREKA PLAZA
18300 SW 137th Ave
Redland

Hot air ballooning is a unique and thrilling way to take in beauty of both the South Florida landscape and its weather. In fact, you actually can't fly when it's windy or rainy. Be aware when you book that flights are subject to postponement or cancellation based on weather. Otherwise, it's a photogenic odyssey.

418 CORAL CASTLE MUSEUM

# 20 PLACES
# TO SLEEP

---

## *The 5 best*
# BOUTIQUE HOTELS

---

### 421 THE REDBURY SOUTH BEACH

1776 Collins Ave
South Beach ⑫
+1 305 604 1776
theredbury.com

This colorful, 69-room sibling to the Los Angeles Redbury packs a lot of personality into its pint-size approach. Guest rooms have lavish touches like 300-thread count Italian linens. The Rooftop Pool and Cleo are both top-tier hangouts.

### 422 GALE SOUTH BEACH

1690 Collins Ave
South Beach ⑫
+1 305 673 0199
galehotel.com

An L. Murray Dixon-designed project from the 1940s, this renovation resulted in 87 chic, minimalist rooms that evoke vintage Capri. Perks include rainfall showers in the marble bathrooms, a rooftop pool and deck, and fabulous Italian food in Dolce Restaurant in the lobby.

### 423 THE BETSY – SOUTH BEACH

1440 Ocean Dr
South Beach ⑫
+1 844 862 3157
thebetsyhotel.com

A wide veranda and greenery-filled lobby are the perfect introduction to this boutique guest house that invites relaxation. Not only does The Betsy pride itself on superior service, it devotes itself to music, art and literary philanthropy; programming takes place daily. And resident LT Steak & Seafood is mouthwatering. One word: popovers.

### 424 THE PLYMOUTH

336 21st St
South Beach ⑫
+1 305 602 5000
theplymouth.com

This Anton Skislewicz-designed building was among the finest of its Streamline Moderne genre in 1940. The same is true now for the redone rooms that rim Collins Park or overlook the restored art deco pool. With inventive Blue Ribbon Sushi Bar & Grill on the premises, there's no need to leave.

### 425 EUROSTARS LANGFORD

121 SE 1st St
Downtown ④
+1 305 250 0782
eurostarshotels.co.uk/
eurostars-langford.html

One of the few boutique properties located in the heart of downtown, this Beaux Arts building – formerly Miami National Bank – combines august history from 1925 with today's high technology. Rooftop bar Pawn Broker features craft cocktails and attracts a Millennial-to-Gen X scene.

423 THE BETSY

## 5 of the best
# ROOMS WITH A VIEW

**426 THE TIDES
SOUTH BEACH**

1220 Ocean Drive
South Beach ⑬
+1 305 604 5070
tidessouthbeach.com

With interiors by Kelly Wearstler and exteriors by Mother Nature, The Tides is positioned to capture every ocean sunrise and sunset. When established in 1936, it was the tallest in Miami Beach. With a recessed façade, tall ceilings and huge windows, it still offers only 45 rooms from which to catch prime views.

**427 CARILLON MIAMI
WELLNESS RESORT**

6801 Collins Avenue
North Beach ⑯
+1 305 514 7000
carillonhotel.com

Perched on the edge of North Beach, the Carillon offers a bastion of beautiful sights that are accompanied only by the sighing of ocean waves. One- or two-bedroom suites allow guests enough space to soak in the views as they also practice the wellness routines they learn from on-staff experts.

**428 MONDRIAN
SOUTH BEACH**

1100 West Avenue
South Beach ⑬
+1 305 514 1500
morganshotelgroup.com/
mondrian

Perched on the lip of land where the General Douglas MacArthur Causeway (I-395) kisses West Avenue, the Mondrian allows cosmic views of ocean and sky. Whether clear or stormy, it's always a performance out there, and every room at this dramatically designed hotel offers a front seat to it.

### 429 SAGAMORE MIAMI BEACH

1671 Collins Avenue
South Beach ⑬
+1 305 535 8088
sagamore
southbeach.com

An all-suite hotel, the Sagamore is heavily invested in the visual arts scene. That's why suites are named after what you might see from them, such as the 'Garden View' – a lush landscape that lights up at night – or the 'Ocean Lanai', where the 750-foot balcony permits precious moments with the beach and ocean.

### 430 INTERCONTINENTAL MIAMI

100 Chopin Plaza
Downtown ④
+1 305 577 1000
icmiamihotel.com

The 34-story InterContinental pre-dates downtown Miami's renaissance. And while the stimulating views of Biscayne Bay have never changed, downtown now includes architecturally interesting arenas, museums, amphitheaters and parks. Even the hotel itself has LED artwork flashing on its side. No matter which direction you look, there's something exciting to see.

429 SAGAMORE MIAMI BEACH

# *The 5 most*
# LUXURIOUS HOTELS

### 431 FAENA HOTEL MIAMI BEACH

3201 Collins Avenue
Miami Beach ⑪
+1 305 534 8800
faena.com/
miami-beach

This independent hotel is stunning in so many aspects it's difficult to list them all. Restaurants by globally-renowned chefs? Check. Design-rich bars and lounges that offer everything from private movie screenings to cabaret entertainment? Oh, yes. Important visual arts imported from Latin America? Indeed. It's a must-stay-to-be-believed kind of place.

### 432 THE SETAI MIAMI BEACH

2001 Collins Avenue
South Beach ⑫
+1 305 520 6000
thesetaihotel.com

Penultimate tranquility exists in this renovated Dempsey-Vanderbilt art deco building, initially designed by famed architect Henry Hohauser. Renowned for its customer service, The Setai never disappoints on any level. Both posh and zen from its rainfall showers and Frette linens to its exclusive spa treatments and culinary concoctions, it leads the beach in luxury.

## 433 THE MIAMI BEACH EDITION

2901 Collins Avenue
Miami Beach ⑪
+1 786 257 4500
editionhotels.com/
miami-beach

The hotel to book when you have an appetite for all things luxury – fare from celebrity chef Jean-Georges Vongerichten; spectacular design; unparalleled spa treatments; and BASEMENT, a nightclub, bowling alley and ice-skating rink. During the day, nestle like a sea turtle on the private-access, 6503-square meter beach or dive into the property's restored, original pool.

## 434 MR. C COCONUT GROVE

2988 McFarlane Rd
Coconut Grove ⑧
+1 305 800 6672
mrccoconutgrove.com

Run by brothers Ignazio and Maggio Cipriani, descendants of the inventor of the Bellini in Venice, this lovely Italian hotel offers 100 rooms and suites with private terraces and views of Biscayne Bay. Book a customized spa service, then cap it off with – naturally – a cocktail at the rooftop Bellini's.

## 435 COMO METROPOLITAN MIAMI BEACH

2445 Collins Avenue
South Beach ⑪⑫
+1 305 695 3600
comohotels.com/
metropolitan
miamibeach

Known globally for personalized, erudite wellness facilities, COMO has one location in the U.S. – in this beautifully preserved art deco building called The Traymore. Added on: A rooftop hydrotherapy pool, steam room, yoga terrace, and signature Shambhala treatment rooms, among other amenities, including a dock that leads to the bay. Locals take staycation here.

## *The 5 nicest*
# HOTEL POOLS

---

**436 THE BILTMORE**

1200 Anastasia Ave
Coral Gables ⑨
+1 855 311 6903
biltmorehotel.com

Renowned for its size – it was once the largest in the world – the Biltmore pool is 2137 square meters. It's also where the original Tarzan, actor Johnny Weissmuller, worked as a lifeguard. For the most luxe experience, rent a cabana and take an outdoor rain shower under native palms after a dip.

**437 DELANO SOUTH BEACH**

1685 Collins Ave
South Beach ⑬
+1 305 672 2000
morganshotelgroup.com/
delano

The Delano is famous for its long, mostly shallow pool, which has cafe furniture actually immersed in it. In addition to admiring designer Philippe Starck's tropically landscaped quirkiness, you can book spa treatments or have a meal and a cocktail next to it. Hotel guests only until 7 pm.

**438 NATIONAL HOTEL**

1677 Collins Ave
South Beach ⑬
+1 305 532 2311
nationalhotel.com

This pair of pools – one more of a square, the other a thin rectangle – includes the longest infinity-edge pool in Miami Beach. Fringed by palm trees and other assorted native foliage that provides shade, the pools are so tempting you might never make it to the beach. *C'est la vida loca.*

### 439 1 HOTEL SOUTH BEACH

2341 Collins Ave
South Beach ⑫
+1 866 615 1111
1hotels.com

Deeply concerned with sustainability, 1 Hotel incorporates design with ecologically sound practices. This ethos extends to the South Pool, the Center Pool, the adult-only Rooftop Pool and the private Cabana Pool, where the day beds and cabanas utilize reclaimed wood and natural fabrics and all views of the ocean are pristine and panoramic.

### 440 FOUR SEASONS HOTEL AT THE SURF CLUB

9011 Collins Avenue
Surfside ⑩
+1 305 381 3333
fourseasons.com/
surfside

This is not just any Four Seasons, and this is not just any pool. The renovated Surf Club was home to Harvey Firestone and his Rat Pack friends. The beachside pool is just an extension of this elegant palazzo. You almost expect a serenade as you lounge by the palm trees.

436 THE BILTMORE

BISCAYNE NATIONAL PARK

# 50 WEEKEND ACTIVITIES

---

# 5 intimate
# WELLNESS FACILITIES

---

**441 BREATHE PILATES**

715 NE 79th St
MiMo District/
Upper East Side ②
+1 786 801 9860
breathepilates
miami.com

This lovely, full-service Pilates studio offers classes and private lessons. But even the classes can feel like individual sessions due to the size of them – they're restricted to the five reformers available. Talented instructors, headed by owner Gretchen Wagoner, and engaging specials also tempt the typical studio jumper to stay put.

**442 INHALE MIAMI**

6310 NE 2nd Ave
Little Haiti ②
+1 786 391 1897
inhalemiami.com

It's hard to tell from the outside just how spacious and restful this urban yoga studio is on the inside. Classes focus on everyone from families to those with autism. Inhale also hosts musical performances, lectures and workshops, all designed to ease stress and enhance quality of life.

## 443 INNERGY MEDITATION

1560 Lenox Ave, #102
South Beach ⑫
+1 305 266 2277
*innergymeditation.com*

Miami's first walk-in meditation studio, Innergy allows those seeking a little bit of space and a whole lot of chill to find it on the spot. Classes range from 20 to 45 minutes; absolute beginners can take an introduction first. No need to worry about special outfits, postures or poses. Take a workshop or a private session.

## 444 FEEL THE HEAL

717 NE 79th St
MiMo District/
Upper East Side ②
+1 305 466 9268
*feeltheheal.com*

Traveling can be tough on the digestive system. So can daily stress. Visit this studio to detox the body through colonic irrigation, abdominal cupping, ear candling and more. Looking for foot ion or liver gallbladder detox? Heal here. Or simply get in bathing suit shape with a cellulite body or mud wrap.

## 445 BODYSENSE

2292 Coral Way
Coral Gables ⑧
+1 305 854 3100
*bodysenseusa.com*

Feel better through medical, postpartum, sports and Oriental foot massages, among other types. Balance your skin and rid it of impurities by way of various facials, including de-reddening and anti-aging. You can even get screened for early breast cancer here through thermography. Whether the wellness is mental or physical, BodySense has you covered.

# The 5 best small
# SPAS AND SALONS

---

### 446 GG SALON & SPA

9063 Biscayne Blvd
Miami Shores ①
+1 305 759 9710
ggsalonspa.com

A full-service establishment for the whole family, the salon is run like a family institution. Everyone loves GG, especially her staff, who you can count on to stay year after year. Services range from traditional to trendy, and products are always organic and wellness-oriented. Book online for convenience.

### 447 BELLEZZA

7245 SW 57th Ct
South Miami ⑨
+1 305 284 0669
bellezzaspa.com

The combination of salon services, spa offerings and med-spa features turn this establishment into an all-day experience. Combine a facial or microdermabrasion with a body scrub and massage, and follow it up with beautifying hair and nail treatments. A dedicated staff diagnoses your skin/hair type before you begin.

## 448 SKIN BY TATUM

1819 West Ave, Unit 1
South Beach ⑫
+1 305 531 5994
skinbytatum.com

Founder Tatum Fritts, who has a lot of education and experience in the skin field, can make you glow. Put yourself in those knowledgeable hands and let them exfoliate, detox, steam, scrub and more. You'll leave with visible results, and some knowledge of your own on how to maintain that radiant exterior.

## 449 ATMA BEAUTY

1874 West Ave
South Beach ⑫
+1 786 216 7510
atmamiami.com

Celebrity stylists, a resident Chihuahua named Rickee Ricardo and a variety of eclectic, interior divisions – including a retail shop selling cool apparel and accessories – in this 650-square meter multi-level space create a distinct non-salon feel. Living room-style stations for hairdressing add warmth and sociability. Services include spray tans, waxing, nail art and med-spa injectibles.

## 450 DANNY DILLON SHAMPOLOGY HAIR

2690 NE 2nd Ave
Wynwood ③
+1 305 576 1530
shampologysalon.com

It's easy to guess that this contemporary, minimalist salon focuses on hair: styling, color, recovery and maintenance. Danny Dillon, working in Miami since 1992, is known for his precision cuts. What's less well-known are the other services you can acquire here, from full-body waxing to eyelash extensions. Credit cards are required for booking appointments.

# 5 things to do in
# BISCAYNE NATIONAL PARK

---

9700 SW 328th St
Homestead ⑬
+1 305 230 1114 x555
*nps.gov/bisc*

451 **DIVE AND SNORKEL THE MARITIME HERITAGE TRAIL**

SCUBA divers and snorkeling buffs get more than their fill exploring 100 years' worth of underwater wrecks. Comprising 6 ships that date back to 1878, the sites can only be reached by boat. The Fowey Rocks Lighthouse, which was supposed to prevent the ships from grounding on the reefs, is also part of the trail.

452 **KAYAK AND CANOE TO THE BOCA CHITA KEY LIGHTHOUSE**

Biscayne Bay is so shallow in spots it's almost like you're paddling in a giant puddle. Don't be fooled. The over 11-kilometer distance to Boca Chita Key to climb the lighthouse, built in the 1930s, is a shoulder-stretching one. Rent at Dante Fascell Visitor Center Wednesday-Sunday or bring your own and launch for free.

## 453 FISH OVER CORAL REEFS

The living coral reefs provide a vast array of species for both sport and dining purposes. But the reefs also pose boating challenges, and the convoluted laws – the park is federal, but fishing and harvesting is taken care of by the state – create others. Check seasons, prohibitions, and licensing regulations before you begin.

## 454 VISIT THE MUSEUM AT CONVOY POINT

The park, 95 percent of which is underwater, actually has four different ecosystems. Learn about them at the museum through multi-media exhibits. Kids can touch everything from bones and feathers to sponges and coral, and adults can admire displays of local art inspired by the park.

## 455 CAMP AT ELLIOTT KEY

The park's largest island has facilities including grills and rest rooms with cold running water. You can make the 27,4-kilometer round trip in a canoe or take the boat that leaves the Visitor Center daily at 8 am and Elliott Key at 9 am. The campsite costs 25 dollars; transportation fees are separate.

# *5 lovely*
# DAY TRIPS

---

## 456 KEY LARGO

Mile Marker #106
The Keys ⑬
*floridarambler.com,*
*fla-keys.com/key-largo*

This large island is home to the historic Key Largo Rock Castle or the century-old African Queen, used on the 1951 movie. Spot wildlife at John Pennekamp State Park, the Florida Keys Wild Bird Center or the Florida Keys National Marine Sanctuary. And swim with everyone's favorite marine mammals at Oceanside Dolphins.

## 457 LAS OLAS BLVD

Fort Lauderdale
*lasolasboulevard.com*

Pleasantly panoramic, the heart of Fort Lauderdale's downtown district is filled with artsy shops, fashionable boutiques and trendy indoor/outdoor cafes and bars. It's slightly more relaxed than Miami's main thoroughfares, but no less fabulous for people watching. Las Olas also hosts annual festivals and art shows.

456 **KEY LARGO**

457 **LAS OLAS BLVD**

## 458 ISLAMORADA

Mile Marker #87
The Keys ⑬
*floridarambler.com*

Islamorada is famous for the Tiki Bar at Postcard Inn Beach Resort & Marina at Holiday Isle; Green Turtle Inn; and Islamorada Fish Company. If you don't feel like drinking or eating, browse the Rain Barrel Artisan's Village – and greet the humongous lobster named Betsy out front. Great photo opp.

## 459 HM69 NIKE MISSILE BASE

AT: EVERGLADES NP
Research Rd
Homestead ⑬
+1 305 242 7700
*nps.gov/ever*

This Cold War military base explains the enmity between the U.S. and Cuba. Great for fans of history and nature both, as the site is close to the Everglades' Royal Palm Anhinga and Gumbo Limbo trails, Pineland Trail and Pahayokee Overlook. Do some or all in a day. Stop first at Ernest Coe Visitor Center.

## 460 ROB'S REDLAND RIOT SELF-GUIDED TOUR

Redland/Homestead
*redlandriot.com*

Get in your car and follow the directives to a dozen spots in the Redland/Homestead farming region. These include Knaus Berry Farm for incredible cinnamon rolls; Schnebly Redland's Winery & Brewery, where fermentation begins with tropical fruits; and Cauley Square, a historic village of antique shops with a quaint tearoom.

## 5 waterways and marinas for
# WATERSPORTS AND FISHING *charters*

461 **OLETA RIVER STATE PARK**

400 NE 163rd St
North Miami Beach ①
+1 305 919 1846
*floridastateparks.org/
park/oleta-river*

Located in the middle of the city, Oleta is known for its outstanding water access. Swim from the 366-meter beach; fish the Intracoastal Waterway; or stand-up paddleboard, kayak or canoe through Oleta River into Biscayne Bay. Ask about tours at the BG Oleta River concession (*bgoletariveroutdoor.com*) or at Biscayne Bay Aquatic Preserves EcoExperience Tours (*EcoExperienceTours.com*).

462 **MIAMI WATERSPORTS COMPLEX**
AT: AMELIA EARHART PARK

401 E 65th St
Hialeah ⑯
+1 305 476 9253
*miamiwatersports
complex.com*

This guaranteed 'Get Up' Rixen cable system wakeboard park is hands-down some of the best water sports fun in town. Beginners can book private, 15-minute instructional sessions first, while advanced riders can go for the double cable system right away. You can also take boat driving lessons and watch pro competitions here.

### 463 MIAMI BEACH MARINA

300 Alton Rd
South Beach ⑫
+1 305 673 6000
*miamibeachmarina.com*

South Beach's 400-slip marina provides plenty of services ranging from yacht brokers to sightseeing tour boats. For SCUBA gear and courses, head into Tarpoon Dive Center (*tarpoondivecenter.com*); for sport or drift fishing charters, check out the options at Bouncer's Dusky 33 (*captbouncer.com*). Find Jet Ski rentals and tours at American Water Sports (*www.jetskiz.com*).

### 464 DINNER KEY MARINA

3400 Pan American Dr
Coconut Grove ⑧
+1 305 329 4755
*miamigov.com/
marinas/pages/
marinas/
dinkeymarina.asp*

The historic home for Pan American Airways 'flying boats', this marina is renowned for sailing lessons and charters. Novices and seasoned sailors alike can appreciate the breadth of instruction and boat selection – and so can those who prefer to just sit back, let others do the tacking and be taken on a tour.

### 465 BILL BIRD MARINA

10800 Collins Ave
Sunny Isles Beach ①
+1 305 947 3525
*www.miamidade.gov/
parks/bill-bird.asp*

Because the marina is sandwiched between the ocean and the Intracoastal, a large fleet of sport and drift fishing boats camps out here, waiting for avid clients who don't like to go very far before dropping a line. A dive boat, boat and Jet Ski rentals and plenty of other amenities are on hand, too.

# *The 5 most beautiful*
# BIKE RIDES

466 **SHARK VALLEY VISITOR CENTER**
AT: EVERGLADES NP
36000 SW 8th St
Miami ⑬
+1 305 221 8776
nps.gov/ever

Pedal around alligators (not sharks) on this 24-kilometer path in National Everglades Park. A variety of the reptiles are usually sunning themselves on the pavement. Don't worry – they're somnolent and not going to chase you as you ride by. Also look for dozens of subtropical bird, amphibian and mammal species while you ride. Rentals available.

467 **RICKENBACKER TRAIL**
Rickenbacker Cwy
Key Biscayne ⑥
www.miamidade.gov/
parks/rickenbacker.asp

From the toll through the islands of Virginia Key and Key Biscayne and Virginia Key, as well as along the beaches. This causeway is the equivalent to a mountain in Miami, and the only elevation where serious cyclists can train. It also happens to be gorgeous, with water sparkling and beaches gleaming on both sides. Do take care to watch traffic, as drivers are not always watching you.

466 SHARK VALLEY

## 468 SNAKE CREEK TRAIL

North Miami Beach ①
miamidade.gov/
parksmasterplan/
library/snake.pdf

From Florida's Turnpike in Miami Gardens to NE 19th Avenue in North Miami Beach. Paved and perfectly flat, this 10,5-kilometer path is a pleasant bike ride for the entire family. It twists and turns by a canal enhanced with fitness stations and shade shelters. Park at Barry Schreiber Promenade (NE 172nd St and S Glades Drive) or Snake Creek Linear Park (NE 169th St and NE 15th Avenue).

## 469 OLD CUTLER TRAIL

Old Cutler Rd
and SW 224th St
in Cutler Bay to
Old Cutler Rd and
Cocoplum Circle
in Coral Gables
www.miamidade.
gov/parksmasterplan/
library/OCT.pdf

This stunning, 17,7-kilometer ride takes you through Miami's southern neighborhoods and under the canopies of old ficus and banyan trees. Stops along the route for botany lovers might include Matheson Hammock Park, Fairchild Tropical Botanic Garden and Pinecrest Gardens. Riders should be a little experienced, as the tree roots stipple sidewalks and streets.

## 470 VIRGINIA KEY NORTH POINT TRAILS

AT: VIRGINIA KEY
MOUNTAIN BIKE PARK
Arthur Lamb Jr Road
Virginia Key ⑥
vkbctrails.com

Dedicated mountain bikers will be thrilled to know that even at sea level, you can train on some pretty tough terrain. The 7,5 miles of trails were built and are maintained by private donors, so if you go to enjoy them, consider donating afterward. And do check out the site map before you ride.

# *The 5 greatest*
# GOLF COURSES

---

### 471 MIAMI SHORES COUNTRY CLUB

10000 Biscayne Blvd
Miami Shores ①
+1 305 795 2360
*miamishoresgolf.com*

This 18-hole, country club golf course has both history and reasonable prices going for it. In addition to some gorgeous, subtropical landscaping, there's plenty of wildlife, including an albino fox, that lives here. Non-resident tee times are listed on the site.

### 472 JW TURNBERRY MIAMI RESORT

19999 W Country
Club Drive
Aventura ①
+1 305 932 6200
*jwturnberry.com*

Where else can you play with pink flamingos? They gather, along with swans and ducks, at the water features on these two famed 18-hole courses, originally designed by Robert Trent Jones Sr., then redesigned by Raymond Floyd. They're home to PGA and LPGA tournaments – but also where fledglings can learn to fly.

### 473 MIAMI BEACH GOLF CLUB

2301 Alton Road
South Beach ⑪⑫
+1 305 532 3350
*miamibeachgolfclub.com*

These lovingly groomed greens were once known as the neglected Bayshore Golf Course, built in 1923. Now thriving with a Jim McLean Golf Academy on the premises, it truly fulfills original developer Carl Fisher's dream for it. The club embraces visitors of all ages and also allows installations during Art Basel.

### 474 CRANDON GOLF COURSE

6700 Crandon Blvd
Key Biscayne ⑥
+1 305 361 9129
*golfcrandon.com*

With a stunning backdrop of downtown Miami and a foreground of Biscayne Bay, Crandon practically begs visitors to play golf, if only for the views. Its beautifully kept public course is also one of the hardest par-72 in the state. That seventh hole… well, there's a reason it makes *Golf Digest*. Pros play here.

### 475 GRANADA GOLF COURSE

2001 Granada Blvd
Coral Gables ⑨
+1 305 460 5367
*coralgables.com*

When you don't have much time, try this 9-hole, par-36 course. Debuting in 1923, it's the oldest of its kind in the state. Perfect for beginners or more seasoned golfers who want to get in a few rounds, followed by a meal at the 10th hole, aka Burger Bob's.

472  TURNBERRY ISLE MIAMI

# *5 terrific*
# TENNIS FACILITIES

### 476 CRANDON PARK TENNIS CENTER

7300 Crandon Blvd
Key Biscayne ⑥
+1 305 365 2300
*miamidade.gov/parks*

Hard courts? Yes. Clay? Certainly. Grass? You betcha. That's because these 26 courts, half of which are lighted, are not only for residents and visitors to utilize. The Miami Open presented by Itaú is played here, as well as 14 USTA junior and two USTA adult tournaments. Lessons, classes, camps and more.

### 477 SALVADORE TENNIS CENTER

1120 Andalusia Ave
Coral Gables ⑨
+1 305 460 5333
*coralgables.com*

For a casual but still well-maintained tennis experience, play on these 13 lighted clay courts. They're almost always open, holidays like New Year's Day and Thanksgiving included (although hours may be shortened). Call ahead or check in at the pro shop for a court assignment.

## 478 PENNY SUGARMAN TENNIS CENTER AT SANS SOUCI

1795 Sans Souci Blvd
North Miami ①
+1 305 893 7130
northmiamifl.gov

Hidden on a side street behind a convenience store, this tennis center has more ambition than it appears. Professional trainers, spring and summer camps, and opportunities for USTA junior memberships and teams abound. All ages, including 'tiny tots', are encouraged to play on the 13 lighted (12 clay and 1 hard) courts.

## 479 MORNINGSIDE PARK

750 NE 55 Terrace
MiMo District/
Upper East Side ②
+1 305 795 1834
miamigov.com/parks

Playing tennis in this city park, located next to Biscayne Bay, is an exercise in pleasure. Breezes from the water come in to cool you off no matter how hard you serve, volley and smash it from the baseline. Open 8 am to 9 pm on weekdays and 7.30 am to 6 pm on weekends.

## 480 FLAMINGO PARK TENNIS CENTER

1200 Meridian Ave
South Beach ⑫
+1 305 673 7761

Strategy and fitness clinics and camps for both adults and kids. Events like Guys' or Girls' Night Out. Competitive and social tournaments organized for locals. Retreats designed for corporations. At these clay courts, tennis is a community sport as well as a way to meet new friends.

## 5 fun places to
# PLAY OR WATCH SOCCER

---

### 481 URBAN SOCCER FIVE
1125 NW 71st St
West Little River ②
+1 786 253 2888
urbansoccerfive.com

Formerly Midtown Indoor Soccer in Wynwood, where it operated for a decade, this business is now five indoor, small turf fields in West Little River. Play 5v5 or 6v6 games or tournaments, or try the first hard-floor futsal court in Miami (where you can also play basketball). A bar shows pro games on a wide screen.

### 482 SOCCER CAGE
301 SW 8th St
Brickell ⑤
+1 305 343 1757
soccercagemiami.com

Open 24/7 in the heart of downtown, the 4v4 soccer cage rents between 50 to 80 dollars per hour, depending on day and time. The facility also has larger 6v6 player fields for 100 to 120 dollars per hour. All ages, all sizes, all genders are welcome to form teams and play. The facility also sponsors events and tournaments.

485 THE SOCCER ARENA / BRICKELL SOCCER ROOFTOP

## 483 INDOOR SOCCER PRO

1128 NW 159th Dr
Miami Gardens ①
+1 305 454 0900
indoorsoccerpro.com

Open from 8 am to midnight, this air-conditioned futsal/indoor soccer facility offers the usual youth development training, leagues and tournaments on its three 5v5 fields. As additional features, it provides 'soccer-sitting' – a place to leave your kids for some activity on days off from school and when you need a night out.

## 484 REVO SOCCER DORAL

10395 NW 41st St,
#101
Doral ⑯
+1 305 717 0020
revosoccer.com

Revo claims to have the biggest indoor 6v6 fields and the best, FIFA-approved artificial grass in the city. On a less serious note, it also offers 'glow soccer' and 'lazerball'. Sign kids of all ages up for summer camp and Revo Soccer Academy (ages 3 to 7).

## 485 THE SOCCER ARENA / BRICKELL SOCCER ROOFTOP

444 Brickell Ave,
2nd Floor
Brickell ⑤
+1 305 967 3512
thesoccerarena.com/
listing/soccer-rooftop

The game doesn't get any better than when it's played on pro-style turf on the top of a building in downtown Miami. Lighted, netted and padded courts make sure that no one hurls themselves into – or off – something dangerous, and lounges, locker rooms and concessions add to the overall futbol vibe.

# *The 5 most magical*
# MOON OVER MIAMI ACTIVITIES

---

**486 FULL MOON PADDLEBOARD & KAYAK TOUR**
AT: VIRGINIA KEY OUTDOOR CENTER
3801 Rickenbacker Causeway
Virginia Key ⑥
+1 786 224 4777
vkoc.net

This two-hour paddle, suitable for any experienced beginner, is a stunning way to experience the Magic City. Watch the sun set and the skyline light up with its signature neon and pastel colors from your perch. Then head back to the center to watch the moon reach its full, glittering potential.

**487 FULL MOON YOGA**
AT: DEERING ESTATE AT CUTLER
16701 SW 72nd Ave
Palmetto Bay ⑬⑭
+1 305 235 1668
deeringestate.org/events

History, education and environmentalism are paramount at the 444-acre former estate of industrialist Charles Deering – and so is yoga. Perched on the lip of Biscayne Bay, the property features a unique energy that renowned yoga instructors capture at the height of the moon (and other times). See the calendar for themes, guests and requirements.

### 488 GARDENS BY MOONLIGHT

AT: VIZCAYA MUSEUM
AND GARDENS

3251 S Miami Ave
Coconut Grove ⑧
+1 305 250 9133
vizcaya.org,
deeringestate.org

There are so many ways to experience this elaborate villa, built by James Deering – through guided tours, afternoon tea, workshops, holiday parties, community-based scientific studies. But seeing the carefully manicured gardens via moonlight, with live musicians and local artists performing, is perhaps the most meaningful for the soul.

### 489 'BARNACLE UNDER MOONLIGHT' CONCERTS

AT: THE BARNACLE
HISTORIC STATE PARK

3485 Main Hwy
Coconut Grove ⑧
+1 305 442 6866
thebarnacle.org

The Barnacle was built in 1891 by Ralph Middleton Munroe, one of the first to settle bayside. Now a Historic State Park, the preserved property is host to events, including concerts under the full moon. Take a blanket, picnic and loved ones for the sound and sight of days long gone.

### 490 FULL MOON DRUM CIRCLE

AT: NORTH SHORE
OPEN SPACE PARK

79th and Collins Ave
North Beach ⑩

Founded in 2007, this group (Drum Circle Miami Group) has been drumming on the beach during every full moon, and the public is invited to join. It's an amazing ritual, but there is etiquette involved. Read the list of full moon dates and rules on the group's Facebook page, and be aware this is not a family-style event.

# 10 RANDOM FACTS
## ABOUT MIAMI

## 5 sites to visit
# WHERE FAMOUS SCENES WERE FILMED

---

**491 JIMMY'S EASTSIDE DINER**

7201 Biscayne Blvd
MiMo District/
Upper East Side ②
+1 305 754 3692

This long-running diner, open for breakfast and lunch only, appears in the Academy Award-winning film *Moonlight*, set in Miami. The mahogany-colored booths and checkered curtains are the perfect set for the emotional scene, during which the lead reunites with an influential figure from his past.

**492 BIG PINK**

157 Collins Ave
South Beach ⑫
+1 305 532 4700
*mylesrestaurant
group.com*

Open until late night, this retro diner was originally a collaboration between Michael Schwartz (Michael's Genuine) and Myles Chefetz (Prime 112), today two of the most successful restaurateurs in the city. In the Farrelly Brothers comedy *There's Something About Mary*, it was featured as meeting location for two characters. Chefetz still owns the restaurant.

**493 THE CARLYLE**

1250 Ocean Dr
South Beach ⑫
+1 905 483 6826
*carlyleoceandrive.com*

Among the first art deco hotels to be resurrected on Ocean Drive, The Carlyle Hotel, built in 1939, is symbolic of South Beach. Some of the largest productions filmed there, before and after renovation, include *Scarface*, *The Birdcage* and *Bad Boys II*.

## 494 LESLIE HOTEL

1244 Ocean Dr
South Beach ⑫
+1 786 476 2645
lesliehotel.com

Watching the 1994 comedy *Ace Ventura: Pet Detective* is an architectural history lesson. Because the movie was filmed largely on South Beach, you can spot many art deco masterpieces in their before or after stages of redevelopment. The Leslie, constructed in 1937, is one of the most recognizable.

## 495 SOUTH MIAMI AVENUE BRIDGE

400 N Miami Ave
Downtown ④
+1 305 374 3829
bridgehunter.com/fl/
miami-dade/874664

Built in 1985 and improved in 2015 – now it's bicycle-friendly! – this draw-bridge has been useful. Sure, boats of all types can continue along the Miami River. But film directors who need to map out car races and chases in productions like *2 Fast, 2 Furious* and *Miami Vice* have also cashed in.

493 THE CARLYLE

494 LESLIE HOTEL

# 5
# NEED-TO-KNOW FACTS
## *about Miami*

496 **DRESS CODES**

Because it's very hot in Miami for six months, women sometimes seem to dress in as little as possible, and men do not don dinner jackets even in formal restaurants. That said, the air conditioning in public places can make it chilly. And being shirtless or in bathing suits inside is bad form.

497 **RULES OF THE ROAD**

Miami's roadways are limited with too-few main arteries and near-constant construction. The beaches are connected to the mainland by causeways with drawbridges, creating more traffic. Drivers come from many different countries and don't always obey local laws. Drive defensively and always use a current app or Sat-Nav system.

## 498 PUBLIC TRANSPORTATION AND PARKING

*miamidade.gov/transit, miamigov.com/trolley, miamibeachfl.gov/ transportation, cityofdoral.com*

The Metrobus, Metrorail and Metromover are helpful for moving around on the mainland, especially Brickell/Downtown. Municipalities have their own trolley systems, which is useful in places like South Beach, where parking is tight. Check your car in at beautifully designed garages like the Herzog & de Meuron project on Lincoln Road, then trolley to various destinations.

## 499 TIPPING POLICIES

Leave 18 to 20 percent tip for food/drink service and spa treatments. But always check your bill – some establishments add it automatically. Tip valets a few dollars when your car is returned. Bellhops receive 2 to 3 dollars per bag; door attendants who unload your car or hail taxis, 1 to 2 dollars. For housekeeping, 3 to 5 dollars per night.

## 500 LAWS AND MANDATES

You will see people flaunting liquor and drug laws in places like Wynwood and South Beach, which may lead to imitation. Be clear: Open containers of liquor are not allowed in public outside of bars and restaurants, and marijuana in any form is only legal if you are licensed for a medical marijuana card.

WYNWOOD WALLS

# INDEX

# COLOPHON

EDITING and COMPOSING — Jen Karetnick

GRAPHIC DESIGN — Joke Gossé, Sarah Schrauwen and Silke Van Damme

PHOTOGRAPHY — Valerie Sands — www.vsandsphotography.com

COVER IMAGE — Wynwood Walls (secret 326)

The addresses in this book have been selected after thorough independent
research by the author, in collaboration with Luster Publishing. The selection
is solely based on personal evaluation of the business by the author. Nothing
in this book was published in exchange for payment or benefits of any kind.

D/2017/12.005/9
ISBN 978 94 6058 2097
NUR 513, 510

© 2017 Luster, Antwerp
Second edition, October 2019 – First reprint, October 2019
www.lusterweb.com — WWW.THE500HIDDENSECRETS.COM
info@lusterweb.com

Printed in Italy by Printer Trento.